HUNGER PAINS

CYNTHIA MOE

HUNGER
PAINS

A WOMAN'S GUIDE TO A SPIRITUAL FAST

NAVPRESS®

BRINGING TRUTH TO LIFE

OUR GUARANTEE TO YOU

We believe so strongly in the message of our books that we are making this quality guarantee to you. If for any reason you are disappointed with the content of this book, return the title page to us with your name and address and we will refund to you the list price of the book. To help us serve you better, please briefly describe why you were disappointed. Mail your refund request to: NavPress, P.O. Box 35002, Colorado Springs, CO 80935.

NavPress
P.O. Box 35001
Colorado Springs, Colorado 80935

The Navigators is an international Christian organization. Our mission is to reach, disciple, and equip people to know Christ and to make Him known through successive generations. We envision multitudes of diverse people in the United States and every other nation who have a passionate love for Christ, live a lifestyle of sharing Christ's love, and multiply spiritual laborers among those without Christ.

NavPress is the publishing ministry of The Navigators. NavPress publications help believers learn biblical truth and apply what they learn to their lives and ministries. Our mission is to stimulate spiritual formation among our readers.

ISBN 1-57683-716-5

Cover design by Disciple Design
Cover photo by Dennis Skinner/DeGennaro Studios
Creative Team: Rachelle Gardner, Arvid Wallen, Cara Iverson, Glynese Northam

Some of the anecdotal illustrations in this book are true to life and are included with the permission of the persons involved. All other illustrations are composites of real situations, and any resemblance to people living or dead is coincidental.

Unless otherwise identified, all Scripture quotations in this publication are taken from the *New American Standard Bible* (NASB), © The Lockman Foundation 1960, 1962, 1963, 1968, 1971, 1972, 1973, 1975, 1977, 1995. Other versions used include: the HOLY BIBLE: NEW INTERNATIONAL VERSION® (NIV®). Copyright © 1973, 1978, 1984 by International Bible Society. Used by permission of Zondervan Publishing House. All rights reserved; and the *New King James Version* (NKJV). Copyright © 1982 by Thomas Nelson, Inc. Used by permission. All rights reserved.

Moe, Cynthia.
  Hunger pains : a woman's guide to a spiritual fast / Cynthia Moe.
     p. cm.
  Includes bibliographical references.
  ISBN 1-57683-716-5
  1. Christian women–Religious life. 2. Fasting–Religious
aspects–Christianity. I. Title.
  BV4527.M57 2006
  248.4'7–dc22
                              2005024672

Printed in the United States of America

1 2 3 4 5 6 7 8 9 10 / 10 09 08 07 06

TO TIM

Always and forever

CONTENTS

ACKNOWLEDGMENTS

Deepest thanks goes to my friends and family for their help and support during both the writing of this book and the fasts that preceded it. Special thanks to Jodi Schwen for her extraordinary support and words of encouragement at just the right time, and to Rachelle, Terry, and Cara at NavPress for helping me navigate the publishing waters and making it fun. Most of all, thank you, Tim, for years of patiently and faithfully encouraging me to follow God's calling, regardless of the cost to you. You are a true picture of faith being the evidence of things not yet seen.

WHAT TO EXPECT FROM THIS BOOK

I think it will be helpful for me to say right off what the purpose of this book is and what it is not. What you hold in your hands is a guide to help you learn about the remarkable discipline of fasting. It is structured as a personal journal, written as I moved through the process of a forty-day fast. But the material is not meant for only those desiring to undertake a long vow; I also wrote it for women considering a fast of any duration or for those simply wanting to learn about fasting. In it, there is both practical advice for those new to the discipline and inspiration for veterans of fasting. Let me say emphatically that you do not have to be committed to a lengthy fast to learn from this book. I have written it in a way that will be useful no matter how you approach the topic of biblical fasting.

Fasting has long been one of the most ignored spiritual disciplines given to believers for growth and development, but that is changing. Many believe that God is preparing His bride for a time of extraordinary change and that the resurgence of fasting is one means He is using to purify His body on earth.

Please understand that I am not a "spiritual giant" or one

of those women at church everyone wants to nominate for sainthood. I haven't been to seminary, and I'm not the leader of an enormous ministry. I'm just an ordinary suburban wife and mother, a teacher, and a writer. I felt God calling me to fast several years ago, and I started slowly by fasting for short periods of time. Since then, I've completed seven forty-day fasts, journaling my way through each one.

I had read many books on fasting, but none was written specifically for women. I realized a woman's experience of fasting can be different in many ways from a man's, and it seemed my journals could be useful for other women exploring fasting. I felt God asking me to share my experience through a book, and He opened all the doors for publication. I am excited to walk alongside you on your exploration of the discipline of fasting.

In this book, I describe some of the dos and don'ts of fasting I've learned through experience and study. I've included useful information about health concerns, preparing for a fast, emotional considerations, weight loss, dealing with family and friends while you are fasting, and the countless other questions women ask me. You'll also find a list of recommended resources for learning more about fasting.

However, this book is not a prescription for a successful long-term fast. It is not my intention to spell out a formula you can use to conjure up a neat spiritual experience. There is nothing spiritually worthwhile in trying to make a carbon copy of anyone else's walk with Christ. I follow the same well-trodden path used by countless faithful through the ages, but I do not try to fit my feet into their tracks. My feet were meant to make tracks of their own, and so were yours.

Use this book the way you might use a tourist guide. Look over the information and read the stories. Ponder the Scripture and consider the questions. Then listen closely to the Guide and let Him direct you to the best places to put your feet. After all, it is the capture of His heart that is the ultimate goal of all we do.

There is much to be learned in the wilderness of fasting, and by no means should you expect to learn as much from a book as you will from Him as you tread these ancient paths on your own. I pray your heart and mind will be open to whatever God has in mind for you as you consider following Him into this hallowed territory.

THE DAY BEFORE DAY 1

I panicked the day before I started my first long fast. For a year, I had prayed about whether or not God wanted me to commit to a long fast—one that would test the bounds of my physical strength and spiritual maturity. While seeking God's mind in His Word, reading and rereading every passage on fasting I could find, I participated in fasts of three, five, and seven days. I spent some time on a silent retreat pestering God with the one question that would not go away: *Should I commit to a long fast?* After a year of asking, the answer became soft and certain as a spring breeze: *Yes.*

I committed to a fast that would extend through the forty days of Lent, deeply grateful to God for letting me make such a vow. Excited with all the passion of a new bride, I was eager—and appropriately naive. I told only a few people about my plans, faithful friends who would pray for me and keep the fast secret. I was serious about keeping Matthew 6:16-18 to the letter. I didn't know anyone who fasted, and I didn't know how a forty-day fast was kept. I prayed for direction and made decisions based on the simple faith that God would direct my choices. The fast I felt led to undertake would allow me to have any liquid I wanted but no solid foods. It seemed like such a great idea in the months and weeks leading up to the onset of the vow.

Then, on the eve of the fast, I choked. Driving through town to meet my prayer partner, Diane, at the chapel of the local hospital where we regularly met to pray, the reality of no solid food for six weeks really hit me for the first time. *Was I nuts? Forty days and nights without any solid food?* The idea seemed impossible, ridiculous, insane. *What was I thinking?*

Anxiety sucked the edges of my perception inward, my mind casting about for an escape from my self-prescribed doom. The decision I had made seemed reckless. What would God think of me if I freaked out and pulled the plug less than twelve hours before the vow began?

I turned into the hospital parking lot and parked in a secluded spot away from the flow of traffic. After shutting off the car, I sat for a few minutes clutching my Bible and listening to the rhythmic tick of the cooling engine. *Maybe,* I reasoned, *I should allow myself something solid every day, like a cup of rice—just one cup of rice each day to ward off starvation.* My heart began to pound at the prospect of an escape hatch. I wanted an idea I could cling to, a justification for not following my plan, so I did what most modern Christians do: I began to dismiss complete devotion to God's will as an irrational risk and looked for a safer way to serve Him.

I'll bet all along God meant for me to eat some solids every day, I thought. *He wouldn't really expect me to starve on liquids for six weeks, right?*

Silence.

Squirming in the seat, I let my fingers play across the edge of my Bible's pages. The gilding was wearing off, the shiny gold now flecked with white. The book had taken on a worn, well-loved look. The wind rose and nudged the car, rocking it gently. How something invisible and silent could move something so solid was a mystery. *I must have been wrong about this fast,* I told myself, *because I don't believe I can do what God is asking.*

I sank back in my seat and thought about the reactions of people who knew about the promise I had made: their surprise, their distress on my behalf, their hope. I had deliberately told some people I highly respected about the fast so that it wouldn't be easy for me to back out. Now I was angry at myself for doing so. *Oh, the cleverness of me,* I thought irritably. Outside, the chill wind blew a few dead leaves across the blacktop. The bare trees swayed stiffly against a blank gray sky. Late winter is always so barren. There is nothing, no sense of spring's hope except the implied promise that spring has always come before. Lent first, then Easter. I sighed.

I held my Bible and uttered a prayer, a petition to God to reach through the fray going on in my mind and show me His will, because despite my fear, what I wanted most of all was to do what He wanted me to do. I flipped through the Bible, hoping for comfort. Instead, my eyes fell upon an underlined and oft-read passage:

> *If a man makes a vow to the LORD, or takes an oath to bind himself with a binding obligation, he shall not violate his word; he shall do according to all that proceeds out of his mouth. (Numbers 30:2)*

17

No matter how hard I tried, I could not read that verse any way except the way it was written. My stomach sank as I sat alone in the parking lot, turning my promise to God over and over in my head and wondering how I had gotten to a place in my spiritual life that I thought this fast was a good idea. But ultimately I knew for certain that it didn't matter how I had gotten there. What mattered was my next step.

I closed the Bible and slumped forward, leaning my head against the steering wheel. I took a deep breath. Then, in a small voice, I told God I would do the fast because He asked me to. I no longer knew of any good reason except that one.

Submission is a funny thing. As soon as I gave up my right to find a way out of fasting, a weight began to lift from my shoulders. Tension slid off my frame—tension I did not even know I was carrying. What I needed was the simple resolve to move forward, not the confidence that I could succeed. I found great freedom in facing only one choice: to walk forward into the wilderness.

When You said, "Seek My face," my heart said to You,
"Your face, O LORD, I shall seek." (Psalm 27:8)

- Who is primarily responsible for maintaining the integrity of your vow to fast?

- What is your most basic reason for fasting? What is your most basic emotion toward this discipline?

DAY 1

I woke up this morning to enthusiastic rapping on the bedroom door. "Whasssuho?" I called.

"School's canceled!" my thirteen-year-old daughter, Bailey, announced. "It's forty below zero!"

My husband, Tim, moaned and rolled over, pulling the down comforter with him. I propped myself up and pawed sleep out of my eyes so I could look outside. The sun wasn't up yet, but its rays were seeping over the horizon, revealing a sky of sleepy gray that would soon give way to a peerless blue. The trees were absolutely still. No wind. That meant the air temperature was forty below, which meant school really was canceled, which meant the kids would be home *all day long*.

In the next room, a radio roared to life. The phone rang, other kids calling my kids to be sure everyone had heard the joyous tidings of a snow day. Ten-year-old Liz let out a whoop as Bailey banged on her door and told her there was no school. Our son, Joseph, more mature and reserved at sixteen, bellowed at the girls to shut up so he could go back to sleep. The dog barked to be let out. I flopped back onto the bed, pulling a pillow across my face as I felt my dream of a silent, meditative first fasting day crack to pieces like a shattering icicle.

But hallelujah, the fast had begun!

Lesson number one, then, is that the world does not care about the fast. The faster may be thrilled and feel as though all of creation should pause and consider the wonder of embarking on a wilderness vow, but the world—family, coworkers, Mother Nature, the public school system—is so caught up in its own comings and goings that it simply does not have much interest in what the fasting person is doing. For me, the early death of dreams about passing days in monastic peacefulness and simply embracing the reality of my life is a great stress reducer. Life marches forward despite any one person's plans.

Because the decision to fast is a personal one, the activities of the world around the faster cannot dictate what kind of attitude the faster will have. Everything we do is affected by the pull of the world, but everything we feel must be made to conform to the high calling of Jesus Christ. This is the nature of being *in* the world, not *of* it.

As the sun peeked through impotently and the thermometer inched up toward the minus-teens, I went into town to run errands, and although my original goal had been to spend my time curled up with a hot cup of tea and some worship music, leaving the house wasn't all bad. At least I found some solitude in the car. I noticed that most of the "hunger" I felt wasn't real hunger yet but more a sense of wanting something just because I couldn't have it—the age-old lure of forbidden fruit. I knew I wouldn't feel true hunger until my body used some of the stores of winter fat I'd been compiling since November.

I sipped fruit juice and found myself drinking a good deal of water. The cold, dry air was making me thirsty.

As the day wound down into a frigid winter night, I cleared the supper dishes. I could have made the kids do it, but after having them home all day, I looked forward to solitude in the kitchen. As I wrapped leftovers and rinsed plates, I pondered my state of mind. I was now officially behind in my work and not sure where the time would come from for the extra prayer I needed. Less than twenty-four hours into this journey, I already felt overwhelmed.

I wrestled with a sense of how impossible it would be not to eat for the next forty days. Tim came into the kitchen and leaned against the counter, making idle comments as he watched me. He knows when I am upset—he always knows. An alcoholic with more than twenty years of sobriety under his belt, he has a nose for dangerous emotion. He sipped a glass of milk and waited patiently until I was ready to let him in on how I was feeling. He listened and then rinsed his glass and put it in the dishwasher. He pulled me to him so I could bury my face in his chest and rest there.

"You are not fasting for forty days today," he reminded me. "You have to worry about fasting today, right now. Let tomorrow take care of itself."

Obedience in the moment, the very moment in which I exist—this makes so much sense. I pulled back far enough to look at him, and he kissed my forehead.

I love his wisdom.

All discipline for the moment seems not to be joyful, but sorrowful; yet to those who have been trained by it, afterwards it yields the peaceful fruit of righteousness. (Hebrews 12:11)

- What attitude will the world most likely have toward your fast?

- Pay attention to your feelings the first day of your fast. What was the predominant feeling you had?

- Did you succeed in making time to be alone with God in Scripture reading and prayer?

DAY 2

Rejoicing that school was open this morning despite the fact that it was not noticeably warmer, I played hooky from my office and spent a little extra time in prayer and Scripture. The quiet and the hot coffee were too comforting to part with. Some mild diarrhea started today, and I felt tired. I think the continued frigid weather might have been partly to blame for the fatigue; simply going outside wears me out. My muscles ache. I am thirsty and drinking water constantly. I am hungry but not starved. Breaking the habit of eating is a bigger struggle than dealing with actual hunger.

Around noon I dug my car out from under several inches of snow and coaxed the engine to life so I could make an hour-long drive to pick up material for a project I am working on. The time alone in the car was golden. God seemed very near, and even though it sounds crazy to say this, I am sure He is excited that the fast has started. I found myself talking to Him, sharing random thoughts, even questions. The landscape rolled past. I picked up the material, chatted for a few minutes, and then turned my car toward home. I stopped at the local coffee shop and ordered an old-fashioned soda. Sipping it, I retraced my route home, the only sound the merry purr of the car's heater. The miles passed too quickly.

Here's a new development: Noise bothers me. I am not sure where the sensitivity comes from, but things like loud music, yelling, arguing, and even the dog barking aggravate me. I have been turning things down—the radio, the television, my kids' voices—since school got out this afternoon. I am getting irritable but trying not to unload on the family. It feels like a losing battle. They are starting to avoid me. So, selfishly speaking, this crabbiness might have an upside!

Beginnings are hard for me, but honestly, I would not change a thing. I know I have the freedom to quit this fast right now, today, but I don't want to quit. There is too much joy, too much wisdom to be gained if only I stay the course.

I am trying not to think about the thirty-eight remaining days. I am mad at myself for not having spent more time thinking and praying about this fast before it began, even though I know there is no way to really be ready for Lent. I have to let go of the "should-haves" and face the reality that some things always come too soon.

I wonder whether Jesus knew He would be spending six weeks in the desert fasting when He walked down to the Jordan the day He was baptized (see Luke 4:1-2). The Gospels don't make clear what Jesus knew about His ministry or when He knew it, so it is entirely possible He did not know He was about to enter a fast or that it would take place in the wilderness over a period of forty days with only the Devil for company.

A few years ago, I had the chance to go to the Promised Land. I saw the wilderness Jesus was driven to, the vast hills of white and brown sand boiling across miles of empty terrain with hardly a bush for shade or shelter. There are some rocks and cliffs but mostly sand driven into swirling drifts by the winds that blow across the wild. I don't like the idea that anyone would find himself facing that broad emptiness for more than a month with no time to prepare, but in reality, I don't know how anyone could prepare for survival in such nothingness. Then again, survival was not Jesus' intention —surrender was.

Fasting is about dying, and preparing for death is never really successful. The process of letting go of rights—and dying to the demands of the individual body, will, and mind—is long and onerous. Fasting is about laying to rest individuality to pick up the banner of the church, of community. It mirrors the stages that Elisabeth Kübler-Ross recognized as common to the process of physical death: denial/isolation, anger/frustration, bargaining, depression, acceptance.[1] All of those emotions emerge in the process of learning to fast, but with practice one moves through the stages more quickly. Eventually, acceptance comes more easily.

> *"Father, if You are willing, remove this cup from Me; yet not My will, but Yours be done." (Luke 22:42)*

- Think about Jesus' walk away from the river Jordan. What compelled Him to enter the wilderness alone? How do you feel when you embark on a journey without companions to help you along the way?

- What did Jesus have to face and overcome, both physically and spiritually, in the wilderness?

- How does the fact that Jesus entered into a forty-day fast two thousand years ago affect how you look at fasting today?

DAY 3

No self-respecting couch potato would wake up early one morning and decide to go out and run a 10K. If he did, he would be in trouble very quickly and would almost certainly fail. Instead, he would be wise to start his exercise plan by walking a mile or two and then gradually increase his level of physical activity until he's ready for the 10K. Fasting is to the spirit what exercise is to the physical body. People have different reactions to the word *exercise*—enthusiasm, guilt, dread—but everyone agrees that all people, regardless of their current state of fitness, benefit from an appropriate level of exercise. Fasting is the same way. All Christians benefit from the exercise of fasting, though how their fasts look depends on their spiritual fitness.

While a Lenten fast is powerful, the best way for the discipline of fasting to impact faith is by participating in a fast once a week. A regular schedule of fasting snips the strings that tie our bodies to this world—strings that keep our focus on comfort rather than discipline. The fathers of the faith employed the fast as a means of learning mastery over their physical selves. Martin Luther admitted that his flesh "was wont to grumble dreadfully" against the discipline,[2] but he also acknowledged its necessity.

I first began to practice this discipline as a direct result of a desperate prayer uttered late one night. I had prayed God would help me be obedient to His will and the demands placed on me as a wife and mother. I was not born with a natural inclination toward submission (I defy you to show me a Sicilian woman who is), and God had revealed to me that when asked to yield to authority, I made it my special task to dig my heels into the moist black earth, set my jaw, and glare. I was tired of being held hostage by my own tyrannical behavior. God's response was to give me a great desire to learn how to fast. At first, I did not make the connection between the struggle to fast and the inability to submit—I just did what I thought God was asking me to do.

I started with a simple vow: One day a week, I would consume only two pieces of dry toast and any liquid I desired. After a month or so of maintaining this weekly fast, I realized I didn't need the toast. I could manage twenty-four hours on liquids alone. As time went on, I chose to eliminate milk from my list of acceptable liquids, so clear liquids were my mainstay. I learned what hunger felt like, that it would come at predictable intervals, and that it did not last. I learned there was power in mastering my body's demands. After a lifetime of letting my days be shaped by what I *felt* like doing, I discovered how to say no to my physical self. Being in control of my body felt good.

A year of maintaining a weekly fast spurred my spiritual growth. I realized that for reasons I could not define, abstinence from food led to a more concentrated prayer life, more ease in discerning God's will in specific circumstances, and more calm acceptance of another's will. Eventually, I completed fasts of three, five, and seven days. My body reacted predictably to long periods without solid food, and as I grew accustomed to one level of fasting, I was able to move on to the next.

It is important to note that moving to increasingly difficult levels of fasting has nothing to do with asceticism. As I became more competent at fasting, my need to rely on God's power to get me through the fast diminished, and so did my motivation to take part in this discipline. I am motivated to fast not for the fast itself but to understand how to let go of my self-reliance and cling to God. So my increasing ability to fast on one level actually undermined my reason to do so.

Learning to fast is a process. I do not advocate an extended fast for people new to this discipline. It takes time to learn how an individual's body will respond to an extended period without food. Jesus assumed believers would naturally take part in fasting in the same way they would in prayer and giving, but nowhere in Scripture is it written that we must participate in a forty-day fast. I believe to do so is a distinct calling.

Most people do not need to stay on a long fast in order to learn the lessons the fast has to offer. If you haven't fasted before, start with short periods of time. Eventually, a longer fast may come into play. Self-control is not a celebrated discipline in our culture, so the regular practice of a weekly fast is easily bypassed for less difficult, less physical disciplines. We have trouble seeing how the act of not eating can help build spiritual muscle. We tend to think the age of fasting is a lot like the age of miracles: not really gone but strange, rare, and for only the spiritual elite. Not so. In Scripture, the people who performed miracles were not the spiritual elite; they were sheepherders, construction workers, and fishermen. Jesus chose to be reared by a carpenter rather than a priest.

Don't wait until you are some kind of spiritual superstar to learn how to fast. Do it now while you are in the trenches of an ordinarily earthly existence. Take the first step and simply begin.

"I praise You, O Father, Lord of heaven and earth, that You have hidden these things from the wise and intelligent and have revealed them to infants."
(Luke 10:21)

- My deepest, most heartfelt fear about fasting is . . .

- My deepest, most heartfelt reason for wanting to fast anyway is . . .

DAY 4

More hunger today. Chills have arrived in force, which tells me my metabolism has taken a downturn in an effort to conserve energy. It is still barely breaking the single digits outside, so I have taken to staying indoors as much as possible.

Today I started noticing muscle weakness—a sluggish feeling of being weary and saggy. Tim needed me to help hold a shelf while he bolted it to the wall of his shop, and even though the whole process took about two minutes, it wore me out. After I finished helping him, I took a hot bath and put my pajamas on.

I am vacillating between being glad and being sad that my fast has started. This afternoon I stopped at the grocery store and realized everyone in the store was going to go home with groceries, cook some of those groceries, and eat. I know my desires screech loudly right before they die, so maybe that moment of jealousy was a good thing. Maybe my flesh is getting ready to give up. Yeah, right—like my desires have ever died so easily.

A bad habit is developing. When I feel hungry, I am anxious to find a bottle of juice and guzzle it down. I need to stop doing that. It gives me a stomachache. I try to think back to my previous fasts to remember some of the hard physical things that lie ahead, but I can't think of anything. In the spiritual afterglow of previous fasts I have forgotten. Repeating fasts is sort of like forgetting the pain a few months after giving birth and actually contemplating going through it again.

Anyone who has ever fasted for a long period will tell you the first few days are tough. The body is resisting the changes a fast forces it to undergo. Toxins that hide in fat tissue are released as fat is used for energy, and those toxins make a person feel lousy. The mind is still trying to reconcile itself to the reality of a fast, and irritability grows more intense. It's crucial to get a handle on that. Cranky people make poor mirrors to reflect the glory of Jesus Christ. It would be wonderful to be able to escape to a cloistered monastery during the vow, but most of us cannot withdraw from our lives to fast, so we must be mindful of other people's needs despite our choice to forgo meeting our own.

For I joyfully concur with the law of God in the inner man, but I see a different law in the members of my body, waging war against the law of my mind and making me a prisoner of the law of sin which is in my members. (Romans 7:22-23)

- What physical reactions have you noticed when you have become very hungry in the past? Which are the most troublesome?

- Physical disciplines are physically uncomfortable. How will you respond to the physical discomforts of the fast?

- How do you feel about setting aside your own physical needs to meet the needs of other people during your fasting time? How will you deal with feelings of self-pity or resentment?

DAY 5

This evening Tim and I attended a potluck dinner for people involved in the prayer ministry at our church. We brought store-bought brownies and cookies to share, and I sipped a glass of pineapple juice and seltzer water as I sat next to my husband and several other people at the table. Because it's early in the process, I am not so hungry that watching other people eat really bothers me. These are all friends from church, people who have a basic understanding of fasting, so I don't have to worry about questions as to why I am not eating. Later a woman arrives who also forgoes the meal, and she has just a glass of water. She sits next to me and we chat. This is an easy gig as eating affairs go.

Social engagements during a fast can be awkward because they normally involve food. How a fasting person handles food-related social events depends on both the faster and the event. Big events are easy. If everyone is eating, fasting can be disguised by moving about and visiting with different people, collecting dirty plates, or pouring coffee. I attended a funeral during a fasting time one year and camouflaged the fact that I wasn't eating during the luncheon by helping my three small nieces get their plates ready. In a large group, people will rarely notice whether one of their number has not eaten, especially if that person stays right in the middle of the action. When faced with this kind of social situation, I silently pray no one will notice my abstinence, and God almost always responds by protecting my vow from being detected.

Smaller groups are tougher. People notice if one person in a group of twenty or less is not fixing a plate, and they are rarely shy about asking why. When I am questioned about whether I am going to eat, my stock response is that I don't want anything. Sometimes that is enough to satisfy the curious, but often it is followed by chides just to have "a little something." If I have to, I will tell people that I am fasting. Again, sometimes that is enough, but often it is followed by more questions. I answer the questions honestly, but I don't elaborate unless the person seems to have a genuine interest in knowing more about fasting for spiritual growth.

Matthew 6:16-18 says that we are not to boast about fasting, but some people have taken that to mean that we are never to talk about the fact that we are on a fast. That is not what Jesus said. When He returned from His wilderness fast and His disciples asked Him where He had been, He talked about the experience. He described the temptations He faced. He admitted to feeling weak. He explained that the Father ministered to Him through angels that came to His aid at the end of the fast. If He had not shared this information, we would not know about His fast today.

Jesus' warnings in Matthew 6 were aimed specifically at the Pharisees' behavior, not at the act of fasting. The Pharisees fasted on market days, when they knew the streets would be full, and walked about looking famished so everyone could admire their devotion. That is the modern equivalent of a televangelist going on a hunger strike to prove his worth to God and his television audience. God condemns those fasts as being for men, not for Him. We are told to incorporate fasting into our lives so that on the surface it does not appear anything is different, but we are never told to lie about our fast in order to keep it secret.

Avoid planning a vow when you know social activities will require you to be around groups of people and food. Be sensitive to the needs of others. It may be impossible to avoid all weddings and birthday parties over the course of a prolonged vow, but some celebrations are more important to others and can cause hurt feelings if you are not joining in the feasting that accompanies the event. There is nothing holy about planning a fast if it will build resentment toward you and your faith.

When people found out I was fasting for forty days, most thought it was interesting—maybe a little crazy—but otherwise not that remarkable. Ironically, I have known several people who were most severely criticized for fasting by Christian members of their own families. One friend talked about the fast with her two sisters, only one of whom was a believer. While the unbelieving sister expressed admiration for my friend's devotion to her faith, the believing sister was highly critical.

This criticism from others is not unusual and sometimes takes the form of an out-and-out verbal attack, but more often it is a frown, a sharp rebuke about "not getting carried away," or a mumbled question regarding the quality of the faster's mental health. What causes such negative reactions, especially from other believers? Conviction? Misunderstanding? Some, I am certain, are motivated by an honest concern over the faster's well-being. But most just seem to flow from a dislike of rash devotion — the kind of devotion that drives people to do things like break alabaster vials of costly perfume or choose death over denial of the Lord's name.

You must know why you are fasting, how you are fasting, and for how long. If those decisions are made after deep prayer and meditation, you don't have to provide a lengthy explanation to those who question your reasoning for making this vow. Some will never understand, regardless of what you say; others will see the richness of your time in the wilderness and be inspired to walk more closely with God. Be patient with those who don't understand, and decide early that you are willing to be a fool for Christ.

We are fools for Christ's sake . . . we are weak . . . we are without honor. (1 Corinthians 4:10)

- How do you know about Jesus' experience in the wilderness?

- What does this tell you about the appropriateness of talking about your experiences with fasting?

- How will you handle social situations while fasting?

- What does it mean for you to be a "fool for Christ's sake"?

DAY 6

The hunger is slipping away. My body must have figured out how to pacify its energy demands without relying on my mouth. I feel some sharp hunger pains, but after a few minutes they stop. It is as if somewhere inside, someone flips a switch that tells my stomach it won't get what it needs from my mouth, so scavengers are sent out to pry loose one of the Christmas cookies I have been saving on my hips since December. I am beginning to notice that weight is slipping off my frame and my rings spin freely on more slender fingers. My face looks thinner but not so much that anyone would notice yet.

Weight loss is a big deal to most women who fast. "I feel as though God is leading me to this," they whisper, "but I know I will lose weight, and I want to lose weight. So I don't know if I should fast or not. I think it's a vanity issue."

"Why do you *really* want to fast?" I ask. "What is your most basic reason?"

"Because I want to know God better," they respond.

"Well, then you should fast," I tell them.

The majority of women I talk to about fasting worry that they would be doing it just to get thin. I said, the *majority* of women are affected by concerns that fasting is really about weight loss for them. In other words, this is a lie the Devil is using with great success. There is one essential reason this one lie has been so effective in keeping American women from fasting: We don't understand the true nature of humility.

Humility is nothing more than knowing and declaring the truth. That's it. Humility is not walking around staring at the tops of our feet as if we're not worthy to lift our heads. It is not feeling that we are so unworthy of God's love that we never dare lift our faces to the bright sunshine of His affection. Humility is feeling hopeful and excited about God and His ability to make us new. We get messed up in our understanding of humility because we think it's about how we feel, and especially how we feel about ourselves. It's not. It's about truth—the truth of who we are in Christ, of where our value comes from, of how we are saved. Humility is knowing that the fast is about Jesus and not our waistline. If I need to lose weight, then I will invite Christ into that process also, but that has little to do with fasting. Fasting is a separate issue.

The humble person is not the one who accepts herself as she is; the humble person is so secure in the love of God that she is not really concerned about herself at all.

The truth is, we live in a society that alternately tempts us with too much food and chides us for being fat. The value we give to external beauty is disproportionately high compared to how we value internal beauty, so we allow ourselves to emphasize how we look over who we are. We are not good at practicing self-control, and when we do, it feels so weird that we mistake the joy of success for ungodly pride. In all of these things, we emphasize *ourselves* while forgetting that we live and move and have our being in Jesus Christ and that He expected us to fast.

Fasting is about revelation, about getting a clearer picture of who we are and where we stand with God. Revelation is the most effective weapon against pride. The Devil is outraged when we see ourselves in the light of God's holiness, because humility and repentance follow. The Devil finds a humble, repentant person utterly worthless for his means, so he lies and tells us that fasting, a tool to draw us closer to God, will cause us to become prideful. He immobilizes us with fear. Could anything be more offensive to God than our letting His enemy scare us into refusing to obey Him?

The Devil is a jerk, but he is a smart jerk. He knows how to play on our fears to keep us from pursuing God. If we decide not to fast, he beats us up for being unspiritual. If we decide we should fast, he accuses us of doing it for pride and vanity. He knows we want perfectly pure motives for the things we do for God. But can humans have perfectly pure motives? Honestly, even my salvation was not motivated by pure love. I did love God, but I also wanted to approach God on my own terms. It was the rosy glow of hell against my backside that motivated me to salvation His way, the only way. I wanted to save my neck, and, seeing no alternatives, I surrendered.

Almost all of us are concerned about weight loss being the motive for fasting. If you know that your *primary* motive is weight loss, then perhaps you need to enter a partial fast, maintaining calories while restricting yourself to certain foods, and let God work on your heart. But if you are concerned that weight loss is *one* of the motives you have, you are not alone. Most of us feel the same way, but we can't let it keep us from fasting.

> *Good and upright is the LORD;*
> *Therefore He instructs sinners in the way.*
> *He leads the humble in justice,*
> *And He teaches the humble His way.*
>
> *(Psalm 25:8-9)*

- What motivates you to fast? List your motivators in order of significance.

- What other aspects of your spiritual journey have been influenced by "impure" motivations? How has that affected your journey?

DAY 7

With the kids tucked away safely for the night, Tim and I collapsed into our matching overstuffed recliners to relax in front of the TV. As I curled into a warm ball, Tim stretched out and aimed the remote at the set. He flipped the channel to CNN. I started to cry over news stories of bus bombings in Israel. He switched to the local news, and I cried some more over a report of a murder on the Native American reservation just down the road. Tim gave me an uncertain look and then clicked back to CNN. I sighed heavily and began praying quietly for the president, for his safety, for the load he bears. Tim hesitated before surfing through the channels on a quest for some innocuous fluff that would pacify me. He settled on a reality television show about animal rescues. A cat had been in an accident, and the vet was about to euthanize it. It was more than I could take. Patiently, Tim turned the remote over to me, and I switched the station to the Cartoon Network. Bugs Bunny. Better. It was Tim's turn to sigh as he unfolded the daily paper and left Bugs to the task of entertaining the emotional train wreck he calls a wife.

I don't know what it is about fasting that makes me so emotional, but as the physical discomfort begins to quiet down, emotional tenderness seems to peak. I am accustomed to a moderate level of emotional acuity, but something about this discipline cranks all of the dials to high. Where I might otherwise be the spiritual equivalent of an antenna with hunks of foil balled up on the tips, I mutate into a satellite receiver. The input can seem overwhelming sometimes. Most of the people I know who have partaken of a long vow report similar emotional tenderness.

Trying to stuff overwrought emotions is a mistake, so I let the tears come. If there is something that moves me to tears frequently, I spend some time in prayer over that issue. I ask God to help me see what it is He wants me to learn. It might be an area of ministry He wants to prepare me for, or it might simply be an issue He wants me to be more aware of and pray over for a short season. His reason for allowing me the tears is less important to me than acting faithfully on the gift of a tender heart.

Apparently tears are a normal part of fasting. Christians used to refer to the "gift of tears."[3] Perhaps crying is a gift, a freedom from the emotional defensive layers that we hide under much of the time, layers that we shed during a time of abstinence.

Maybe it's part of the humility of fasting. Maybe it has something to do with the physicality of this discipline. The truth is, I don't know why I get so emotional. And I don't feel miserable, just sensitive. So though I am not a weeper by nature, I become one for a few weeks.

Why are you in despair, O my soul?
And why have you become disturbed within me?
Hope in God, for I shall again praise Him
For the help of His presence. (Psalm 42:5)

- On a scale of 1 to 10, what is your usual level of emotional sensitivity?

- During a fast, does your level of emotional sensitivity seem to increase or decrease? Why do you think this occurs?

- Read Psalm 56:8. What does God do with our tears? Why do you think this is?

DAY 8

For every person who has asked me about doing a fast from food, there have been at least two who wanted to give up something other than food and call it a fast. There is a growing movement of abstaining from things other than food in order to devote time to seeking God. Some people go into a fast of silence, taking time apart to spend a day without speaking or listening to anything besides the sounds of nature to better hear the still, small voice of God. The youth group at my church engages in an annual media fast, in which the kids do not watch TV, listen to the radio, or see a movie for six weeks. The media fast gives them time to think about the power they give those sources to influence their minds and hearts. Some people have legitimate medical conditions that keep them from food fasting, in which case it's perfectly appropriate to choose something else to sacrifice for God. Usually people give up good things, harmless things that are not evil. Giving up something good can be a profound sacrifice designed to carve out more space in one's life so that Christ can fill it.

My husband is an avid hunter. He loves to hunt anything that moves. Much of the year, he is either returning from a hunt or getting ready to leave for one. But some of the most special times I remember in our years of marriage have been times he has voluntarily given up a hunting trip just to stay home with me. He gives up something he deeply loves and gives me that time as a free expression of his love for me. It makes me feel cherished as a wife and as a person when he gives up another love for my sake. I can imagine Jesus feeling the same way. It isn't what we are letting go of; it is what we are pursuing: His heart.

As more items are added to the growing list of things we fast from, it is important to clarify some terminology in order to understand what God considers a fast. While it is appropriate to make sacrifices for God, these sacrifices may not all fit the biblical description of a fast.

First, giving up sin is *not* a fast. I grew up in a church where many of us made vows during Lent to give up things we should not have been doing anyway and called that a sacrifice. I remember playing with the idea one year of giving up alcohol for the forty-seven days from Ash Wednesday to Easter Sunday but deciding that would be too hard. Instead, I gave up chocolate and kept the local bars busy. Abstaining from vice is not a love offering to God; it is a fundamental issue in your Christian walk. Fasting will help you break bad habits, but breaking a bad habit is not a fast—it's basic obedience to the Word of God.

Second, if you make a decision to hang on to sin and are not growing and changing through the pursuit of Jesus Christ, your fast will not be a pure, powerful sacrifice. In Isaiah 58, God asks the Israelites why they are surprised He is ignoring their "holy fasts" while they cheat their workers, fight with one another, and ignore the needs of the poor. He tells them to live their lives in wholehearted, generous obedience to His Word and then He will regard their fasting.

If you have a specific sin in your life that you cannot seem to control, then fasting and fervent prayer can help break the power of sin in your life. But if you have a sin you intend to coddle and guard, then your energy would be better spent praying that God would send you the gift of hatred for that sin so that you would want to be set free. Remember that the same God who prescribed the fast spoke these words through the prophet Samuel:

> *Has the LORD as much delight in burnt offerings*
>   *and sacrifices*
> *As in obeying the voice of the LORD?*
> *Behold, to obey is better than sacrifice,*
> *And to heed than the fat of rams.*
>   *(1 Samuel 15:22)*

Third, when the Bible talks about fasting, it is talking about abstaining from food. Scripturally, a full stomach is symbolic of rebellion. Of all the things God might have chosen to withhold from Adam and Eve in the Garden of Eden, He told them not to eat a specific fruit. He might have forbidden them from going to a specific section of the garden, or from picking flowers from a certain plant, or from talking to serpents—which, in hindsight, might have been a fine idea—but instead He told them not to eat one specific fruit from one specific tree. The essential symbol of rebellion was the taking and eating of something forbidden.

Food reappears as a symbol of rebellion over and over again in Scripture. During Old Testament times, God repeatedly warned Israel not to forget Him once they moved into the Promised Land and got a bellyful of its richness. Look at the warnings found in Deuteronomy:

> *When the Lord your God brings you into the land which He swore to your fathers . . . and you eat and are satisfied, then watch yourself, that you do not forget the Lord who brought you from the land of Egypt, out of the house of slavery. (6:10-12)*

> *He will give the rain for your land in its season . . . that you may gather in your grain and your new wine and your oil. He will give you grass in your fields for your cattle, and you will eat and be satisfied. Beware that your hearts are not deceived, and that you do not turn away and serve other gods and worship them. (11:14-16)*

> *For when I bring them into the land flowing with milk and honey, which I swore to their fathers, and they have eaten and are satisfied and become*

prosperous, then they will turn to other gods and serve them, and spurn Me and break My covenant. (31:20)

Of all the things God might have pointed to as a warning of impending rebellion, He chose a full belly. What is the hold food has over us that gives it the power to lead us away from God? I don't know the answer to this question, but I am impressed by the number of people who approach me with their ideas of what they can give up instead of food. More than anything, we don't want to let the groceries go.

The Israelites said . . . , "If only we had died by the LORD's hand in Egypt! There we sat around pots of meat and ate all the food we wanted, but you have brought us out into this desert to starve this entire assembly to death." (Exodus 16:3, NIV)

- How do you feel about the idea of going without food? What happens physically? Mentally?

- Based on the Scriptures discussed, why do you think God uses food as a symbol of rebellion?

- What food do you "worship"? What do you plan to do about that now that you have acknowledged it as fact?

DAY 9

One of my girlfriends heard a radio talk show on the topic of fasting. A man who had maintained a fast for forty days drinking only watered-down juices was being interviewed. During the course of the interview, people were calling in with different questions and comments, and one irate caller made a point of dialing up the radio station to berate the man for drinking juice during his fast. The caller claimed the man had not done a "real" fast because he drank juice.

No standard for how a fast is supposed to be observed is given in Scripture. When the Bible talks about fasting, it sometimes describes a time when the faster consumes nothing but water. We assume this to be true of Jesus' fast because at the end of it, He was hungry but not thirsty. At times of national crisis, the Israelites would sometimes abstain from both food and water, as was the case in Esther's day (see Esther 4:15-16). Daniel entered three weeks of fasting in which he did not eat any meat or drink any wine, and at the end of the three weeks he was given an astounding revelation from God (see Daniel 10–12).

Traditionally, spiritual fasts consist of complete abstinence from food but not water. Maintaining a twenty-four-hour water-only fast once a week is a great idea, but I am not willing to tell another believer who is living in the grace of the Cross of Jesus Christ that her act of devotion is somehow lacking if she chooses to have broth, juice, or other liquids when fasting. Judging another person's act of devotion to Christ is arrogance to the highest degree, and I doubt Jesus would appreciate that from me.

Jesus expects us to fast, but He didn't provide details on how a fast is supposed to look. In order for me to know what His desires are, I go to Him in prayer and ask Him to reveal details of how He wants me to fast, when, and for how long. I consider what I need to do in terms of the life I live, consulting the calendar to see whether there are special occasions or times of stress that might affect when my fast should take place. I avoid times of special celebration, such as Christmas or Easter, vacations, or planned visits by company. Then I plan a fast according to what I understand He would have me do.

But what if I misunderstand Him? I'm so happy God never feels shy about correcting me when I've strayed from the path He has set for me! One year as I planned a fast, I recognized there were going to be more demands on me than usual during that period. I decided it would be wise to do a less stringent fast, allowing myself protein drinks and milk. Several days into my fast, I began to feel convicted, and I sensed something was wrong. I spent extra time in prayer, seeking His will and asking specifically for His help in knowing how to be obedient. It quickly became clear that God didn't want me to make the fast easier on myself and that I was to return to a clear-liquids-only fast. Once I did that, the feeling of conviction disappeared.

Make sure to let God in on the planning process of your fast and listen to His voice even if He seems to be telling you not to fast at all for a season. A friend who planned to enter a long Lenten vow called me to say that as he prayed, he kept feeling that God was telling him *not* to fast. My friend was confused and frustrated by that answer. I advised him to listen to what he understood God to be saying and wait. He waited. About two weeks into the vowed fasting time, my friend's father died very suddenly. Reeling from a bout of hectic travel, arranging a funeral, and mourning the loss of his dad, my friend told me how grateful he was to have been spared the fast. He had enough to manage just plowing through the grief that drifted up every day.

Our view is so limited. Listen to the One who sees the whole horizon with perfect clarity and cares about the success of your vow. He won't steer you wrong.

> *He, your Teacher will no longer hide Himself, but your eyes will behold your Teacher. Your ears will hear a word behind you, "This is the way, walk in it," whenever you turn to the right or to the left. (Isaiah 30:20-21)*

- Have you felt tempted to judge other people's fasts because of the types of things they were allowing themselves to consume? What causes those thoughts to arise in you?

- What steps have you taken to discern what type of fast would be appropriate for you? What is your level of certainty about this decision?

DAY 10

I went to the grocery store tonight, something that is always traumatic for me during a fast. The electric-blue overhead lights and bright, cheery aisles stuffed with mounds of gastronomic delights have always given me a sense of comfort, but not tonight. I walked through the bakery, and the scent of fresh bread made my stomach rumble. I made it past the snack and chip area only to catch myself staring at lovely bricks of thick yellow cheese in the dairy aisle. Although I no longer feel hunger very often, the cheddar just looked so good.

Before I had a chance to feel too sorry for myself, I grabbed the milk I had come for and made tracks to the checkout counter. I did not look to the right or the left as I waited in the express lane. I marched out of the store into the vapory white light of the parking lot, the dark sky above showering fat snowflakes like goose down. I got to my car and sat in the quiet for a moment before I started the engine, chuckling at myself. The way I had bolted out of the store, security probably thought I was shoplifting, but I didn't care what anyone thought. I had done my best to follow the biblical prescription for dealing with temptation: I ran away.

During a fast, putting food in my mouth is not a real choice to me. That ceased to be an issue ten days ago, but I still believe it is utterly foolish for me to deliberately stay where temptation is going to keep nagging at me. It is only a matter of time before that pull toward sin wears me down, and even if I don't give in to the act, I resent God because I feel obligated to keep the vow I willingly made to Him. I am too old to have illusions about my ability to withstand temptation. I just have to leave.

A few years ago, a friend who had embarked on a long fast approached me with a confession. She had been alone in the house, cleaning up the kitchen after her husband left for his job on the night shift at the local power plant. She had made chicken for supper, and a few pieces were in the refrigerator. As she loaded the dishwasher and wiped down the table and countertops, she kept thinking about that chicken. Her husband had told her it was very good. She emptied and rinsed the sink and then took her time giving the stove one last wipe. And that chicken—well, that chicken was still in the refrigerator.

You can guess what happened next. She ate some chicken. And felt terrible about it. And ended up with a stomachache. She told me she didn't know why she had eaten the chicken, because even though she was a couple of weeks into her fast, she really wasn't hungry when she ate it. It didn't even taste good. We prayed together, and she confessed her sin to God. She resumed her fast and finished weeks later. I am not sure whether she ever identified the root cause of her lapse. It wasn't that she was alone in the house or that chicken is irresistible; it was that when she was in the kitchen and temptation arrived, she lingered.

I have learned it can be devastating to push yourself to see what you can handle in terms of temptation. There is nothing for you there except the potential for catastrophic failure. Life and the Devil will see to it that you are tempted enough without a foolish predisposition toward seeking out and playing with those foods, things, or people who tempt you. Just get away.

Making matters even more difficult, food is not the only, or even the biggest, temptation that will prey on my mind during a fast, and the Devil will take any opportunity to distract. Being especially aware of what music, movies, and television I expose myself to during the fast is extremely important. This is a great time to submerge myself in God's Word through Bible reading, listening to worship music, and spending protracted time in prayer.

I have a friend who started having an affair during a fast. Before his fast, he had done everything right. He found people to pray for him. He spent time in prayer to confirm that a long fast was God's desire for him. He prepared physically, completing several shorter fasts before the onset of the longer one. When he started the vow, I checked in with him regularly, and he said things were going well. It was not until six months later that I found out he was having an affair and that it started in the midst of his forty-day vow.

It was such a contradiction—a set time devoted to seeking God's face, the lying and sneaking that are always part of extramarital relationships—but it showed me what dreadful temptation awaits in the wilderness. When the Devil met Jesus at the end of the Lord's long vow, food was only one of the baits he used to try to trip Jesus up. The Devil also used the promise of great power and an opportunity to snatch immortality without first tasting death. Jesus passed the test perfectly, but my friend didn't, and many of us won't.

We are remarkably easy to figure out, and the Devil has spent eons learning how to look for human weakness. When we fast and our defenses are down, we can easily trip over lies we would normally recognize a mile away. We have weaknesses, the Devil knows it, and he has no respect for the fact we are supposed to be enjoying a time of special fellowship with our Lord. If he can ruin that time, so much the better.

Do you know where you are weak? When you fast, you are likely to find out. Your weakness is for that forbidden thing you find lurking in the wilderness, the fruit you know you can't touch but that now looks so irresistible. It might be a person. It might be a relationship. It might be sex, or shopping, or envy. It might be food, after all. But it will be something, and you need to keep your eyes open. You will know you are in danger if you find yourself rationalizing your desire to linger and gaze at the bait when you know you ought to turn on your heels and leave a long dust trail as you flee from destruction.

The hallmark of a wise faster is vigilance. Never let your guard down. Don't move even a small step in the direction of something you know is sin. Be on guard about what you listen to, what you see, and who you spend time with. If you find yourself struggling, meet with a person you trust, confess your struggle to her, and ask her to pray for you right on the spot. This is like guerilla warfare, and during a time of guerilla warfare, hesitation can be fatal.

No temptation has overtaken you but such as is common to man; and God is faithful, who will not allow you to be tempted beyond what you are able, but with the temptation will provide the way of escape also, so that you will be able to endure it. (1 Corinthians 10:13)

- How have you dealt with temptation in the past?

- Read Genesis 39. According to this passage, what is the biblically prescribed way of dealing with temptation?

- God never tempts us (see James 1:13), so why did Jesus teach us to pray, "Do not lead us into temptation," in the Lord's Prayer (Matthew 6:13)? (Hint: God can see sin from a distance, while we can see only what is in front of us.)

- Think of something that you know represents a temptation for you. How will you avoid that temptation?

DAY 11

Sitting alone while the house sleeps, I gaze at the clock as it crawls toward the end of another day of this vow. Today—much of this week, actually—I have labored not to feel the pain of my fast, bobbing and weaving around the discipline like a reluctant boxer determined not to take a punch. I drink juice before hunger pains start, heading off the weakness. I convince myself that I should be allowed extra privileges in avoiding my work and that everyone should be patient with me because of my fast. I'm becoming an ill-tempered, demanding penitent. I am not really hungry, but I am not satisfied. And the idea of twenty-nine days remaining feels like a narrow, black hole I must crawl through.

Whining apparently reaches heaven and wears God out, so tonight He showed me something. I sat at my computer to kill some time online and came across an electronic journal posted by a man who completed a forty-day fast during the summer of 1998. Each entry he made rang with a deep, joyous sense of privilege that he felt toward God for allowing him to fast. He wrote of the struggles honestly but almost dismissively, as if the physical ache of fasting was hardly worth mentioning. Instead, his focus was on the delight of being quieter, weaker, and more open to God than he had ever been. He wanted to fast. He loved fasting—or at least what fasting was doing for him. He made me long for what he experienced. My experience thus far felt cheap and naked in comparison.

I read in wonder, trying to discern why his experience was so different from mine. He spoke of drinking fruit juice morning and night and vegetable juice in the afternoon. He said they tasted great. *Great?* I am already so tired of juice it makes me want to gag.

So it hit me. I am drinking juice out of abundance: gulping it, slurping it, lapping it up to avoid feeling hunger. He was drinking juice out of his lack: having only a little bit when he was very hungry so that he appreciated every sip. This isn't an issue about juice consumption; it's about heart position. I am fasting and trying to avoid the results of fasting. He fasted and embraced the pain and was blessed deeply. I am the one who is struggling.

The habit of my life—of most lives—is to avoid pain at all costs. It isn't that Jesus wants us to feel pain; it's that the pain is not the point. Sometimes following Him means walking toward pain. Fasting trains me to follow Him regardless of how I feel. If I refuse to follow Him when He moves in a painful direction, I will lose sight of Him.

Of course, it is also true that if I become an ascetic who loves the pain rather than the obedience, I will still lose sight of Him, thrashing in the brambles as He passes by on higher ground.

I need to stop writing this and go and spend some extra

time in prayer. God wants a commitment that is more about Him than about me, and it will take time alone with Him to figure out how to be a part of *that* fast.

> *Being found in appearance as a man, He humbled Himself by becoming obedient to the point of death, even death on a cross. (Philippians 2:8)*

- Read Hebrews 5:8. How does the fact that Jesus had to learn obedience through suffering change the way you look at suffering in your own life?

- How would you describe how your feelings changed about the struggle of fasting once you made up your mind to accept the physical discomfort that accompanies the vow?

- How will you respond to people's questions about whether or not fasting is an ascetic practice?

DAY 12

Today has been a good day. It seems the determination to accept hunger and discomfort has caused me to feel fewer hunger pains, a fact that makes me wonder how much of my misery has existed only in my head. Ironically, with the decrease in hunger pains has come an increase in nausea. This queasiness isn't severe enough to be debilitating, just a nuisance. A little juice is enough to ease the discomfort, so I assume nausea is my stomach's new response to hunger. Charming.

I decided to confront food and hunger head-on, so I spent some time today cleaning my kitchen. The cupboards and refrigerator were loaded with mostly eaten packages of stale food. I pulled the garbage can out into the middle of the kitchen floor and began lofting rumpled and dusty packages into it. At first it pained me to throw food away, even things that clearly never would be eaten by anyone in my household. I diagnosed that pain as greed. I do not want to be a poor steward of what I have, but this was not about stewardship—it was about sin. As packages filled the trash, I felt a new sense of freedom.

People often ask me if I have ever been tempted to cheat when I am alone. Tempted? Sure, every day. But have I stuck some food in my mouth and eaten it, knowing that no human would be the wiser? No. That I never have done. No matter how strong the temptation, something always stops me from crossing the line of wanting the food to actually taking it. I think it is the prayers of the people who know I am fasting that guard me. I know of a few people who have crossed the line and eaten food during a time of abstinence. They all report essentially the same experience: The food tastes terrible, they find themselves feeling angry for failing, and they end up on their knees asking Jesus to forgive them. They repent and then reenter the fast with a new resolve to finish strong. They find out what millions of us learn again and again: The fruit of temptation is bitter, and it never delivers on its promise of fulfillment for very long.

My friend Jackie tells a story about a long fast she completed several years ago. A bubbly pastor's wife, she embarked on a fast to pray for the struggling, embattled church her husband was leading. One day about halfway through her fast, she decided to clean out her kitchen cupboards. Jackie is just shy of being five feet tall, so she uses a stool for things most of us could do from ground level. But even the stool was not tall enough for her to reach the top cupboard, so she climbed onto the countertop and stood stooped over with her neck cranked sideways to keep from knocking her head on the ceiling. From that precarious position, she could clean the topmost cupboard. She set about removing cans and boxes and bags of food, wiping the shelves clean with a damp rag. She felt good. She felt strong. The boxes and bags and cans of food did not tempt her.

Then she saw it.

Tucked back in the corner of the highest shelf was a lone

saltine cracker. Sometime during the endless months and years of snacks and meals, this one cracker had escaped its cellophane and had come to reside on a lonely stretch of shelving in the nether regions of Jackie's kitchen cabinet.

There she stood, alone in the house, perched on the cupboard with her head cranked at a right angle, face-to-face with a dusty cracker, and twenty days of fasting fell in on her like a cave wall. Jackie was *hungry*. She picked the cracker up and carefully dusted it with her finger. Tempting little flecks of salt glittered like fool's gold. She sniffed it. It smelled of ancient flour and household dust. She wanted to eat that cracker more than she had ever wanted anything. She was alone. No one would ever know. She could have the cracker and keep the secret, and no one would ever be the wiser.

But midway between the shelf and her mouth, her hand stopped. Something at the periphery of Jackie's vision caught her attention. Bags. Boxes. Cans. An abundance of good, tasty, relatively fresh food was spread out all over the counter space. The countertops were heaping with bounty. The refrigerator was full. There was plenty of food. She did not have to settle for a stale cracker.

Jackie tossed the cracker in the trash, and in that moment, she understood two things. One was that the things that most often tempted her were not the obvious things but the unexpected. She knew how to defend herself against the vegetables and soups and muffins, but she was most endangered from the stale cracker—the small, discarded, insidious temptation tucked deep in the corner, waiting to be stumbled upon in a moment of weakness. The other lesson was how completely her fast was between her and God and no one else. She easily could have eaten the cracker, and her only witness would have been God. But God is the only witness who matters.

"Why are you angry? Why is your face downcast? If you do what is right, will you not be accepted? But if you do not do what is right, sin is crouching at your door; it desires to have you, but you must master it." (Genesis 4:6-7, NIV)

- Read 1 Corinthians 10:13. After reading Jackie's "Temptation of the Stale Cracker" story, think of a time when you were faced with sudden, unexpected temptation. Did you succeed in resisting the temptation, or did you fail? What did you do right, and what should you have done differently? Summarize your story.

- Read Isaiah 38:17. What does this verse say to you about how God regards your failures once you have repented of them?

DAY 13

Something is definitely happening. Things are so quiet. *I* am quiet, inside. It is as if somewhere in the back of my mind on the outer border of my consciousness, a radio had been playing with its tuner set to static. There was a blizzard of noise that had roared for so long that I had hardly been aware of it. Today Someone came along and snapped that baby off. What a relief. Thank You, Jesus.

This is such a contrast to the irritation at loud noises that plagued me for a week. It is not the product of what is happening around me, because though I still prefer silence, even loud noise does not shake this peace. It's a quietness so real that it is almost palpable, almost empirical, yet it flows up from a source on the inside. The world cannot squelch it, cannot pry it loose.

Now that the noise is gone, I am trying to discern where it was coming from. Part of it is the result of my body giving up on its demands for food. Giving up my right to feel full has been a mighty relief, but this noise didn't start with my fast. It has been there as long as I can remember. Perhaps it is the grinding dissidence produced by the frustration I feel about failing to be who I want to be. My life is so much plainer, my faith so much weaker, my godly walk so much more human than I had planned. I want to believe that somewhere out there is the future of my dreams, but today is made up of tossing seeds of faith into a giant, swirling chasm of the unknown. That which I long to be I am not, and that which I struggle to escape hangs on me like body odor. And somehow God reaches through the wail of that strife and—*flick*—just that quick shuts it all off.

It feels like rest. My mind was harassed by sound for eons, and, hallelujah, now that harassment has come to an end. The air feels heavier, rich and pregnant with hope and—could it be?—God's own presence. I feel a sublime peace.

The prophet Elijah would understand this feeling of being rescued from earthly racket by the Prince of Peace. After fleeing the chaos of Carmel (see 1 Kings 18:22-40), he hid himself in the deep darkness of a cave and stood listening to all of the normal sounds of this world: the howling wind, the raging storm, the roaring fire. He recognized God in the stillness because stillness is so alien to what we know (see 1 Kings 19:11-13). It has to be supernatural. Nothing of this world breeds deep peace. If the price of eating again in twenty-seven days is having that interior noise turned back on, I am not at all sure the trade is worthwhile to me.

Speak, Lord. Your servant can hear You now.

"Peace I leave with you; My peace I give to you; not as the world gives do I give to you. Do not let your heart be troubled, nor let it be fearful." (John 14:27)

- What kinds of noise do you hear during the course of your day? List some of the sources of noise you are exposed to. Which of these sounds might be eliminated to help you cultivate a quiet spirit?

- The Bible tells us that God defines a beautiful woman as one with a quiet and gentle spirit (see 1 Peter 3:4). How are you doing on this attribute?

- Spend some time—even if only five minutes—alone today. Ask God to protect you from voices that are supernatural but not divine, and invite Him to speak to you. Quietly listen. What thoughts emerge out of this quiet time?

DAY 14

I must be in a state of grace: energetic and happy, rarely hungry. I feel light and joyful, and God seems so very near. When hunger pains come, I offer the hunger to Him as a sacrifice of praise and ask Him to use it to conform me to His image. It seems my stomach stops growling before I even finish the prayer. I don't know if I am growing in His image or not, but I am willing to trust Him on that.

Right now I am living primarily on orange juice mixed with seltzer water, apple juice, soup broth, a lot of water, and coffee. I am sure the health-food gurus would nod approvingly until they got to the part about the coffee. It's not exactly healthy, but fasting or not, I consider it a staple.

I wish I looked as good as I feel. The skin on my face looks saggy, like a balloon that has lost some of its air. I found a magnifying mirror and looked closely at my skin in the sunlight coming through the bathroom window. I will never do that again, fasting or otherwise! My hips are getting narrow, and my stomach is flatter, though it still has an alarming jiggle that was not there a year or two ago. My underwear drawer is divided into "skinny" undies and "fat" undies, and right now I am comfortable in my skinny undies.

My body aches sometimes. My muscles hurt. According to

some of my health books, it is most likely because toxins are working their way out of my system. Judging by my breath, the toxins have all worked their way to my tongue. It has built up a layer of disgusting white sludge, and my breath is hideous. The books say this is the result of the overprocessed rubbish packed on my frame being burned for fuel, kind of like a junk-food penance. I feel sorry that the people around me also have to be afflicted by my breath, but I guess that's the nature of sin: It boomerangs no matter how hard one tries to contain it.

All of this shedding of crud that my body is doing right now is gross but healthy. My body is unloading junk that might cause a problem sometime later. It is not a secret that fasting is physically good for a person.[4] There are places you can go to fast for days or weeks in order to clear out toxins from your body, a practice some cultures have taught for hundreds of years.

Tim likes my svelte new look and has taken to offering me fashion advice. I am enjoying the extra attention rather than judging it—he might as well enjoy this process because he is taking up slack around the house to allow me to be on my fast.

The idea that the body is just a "shell" that is less important and less lovely to God than the spirit is not a biblical one. God loves flesh and bone, so much so that part of His promise to us is the resurrection of these human bodies. He expects us to tend to our physical selves and balance the care of the body with the nurturing of spiritual growth and intellectual knowledge.

How did the ascetics miss this? How did the gluttons?

For you created my inmost being;
you knit me together in my mother's womb.
I praise you because I am fearfully and wonderfully
made. (Psalm 139:13-14, NIV)

- What changes do you notice in your body after some time without solid food?

- What do these changes tell you about how your lifestyle is affecting your physical body?

- The poetic book of Song of Songs is believed by some to be an allegory for how God feels about us, His church. Read Song of Songs 7. How does that chapter's words change the way you see the stewardship of your physical body?

DAY 15

Some days I wonder why I'm really doing this. Okay, a lot of days I wonder why I'm doing this. I know the reasons I *wanted* to fast: to get closer to God, to honor and glorify Him, to find a balance between my spiritual life and my physical life, to focus on some specific areas of prayer, to clear away the fog that keeps me from seeing where God wants me to be working in my life. I guess I wanted to feel holier. But the sad truth is, I don't feel holier. Actually, I feel a lot less holy than I did two weeks ago.

Right now I don't feel closer to God. I don't think I can hear Him any better than usual. I don't feel more like praying, and, if anything, I feel more sensitive to just how completely out of balance my life is. I am gaining a clearer perspective, but frankly, I don't like it at all. A bit too much honesty here. Forget reality—bring on the delusion.

David wrote in the psalms about humbling himself with fasting. I always saw humility as something David actively sought, not as something he might have stumbled onto as a result of the fast. I wanted to become more humble, but I don't feel humble—at least I don't feel like I had imagined humble would feel. I just feel frustrated with my inability to reach God and nauseated at how helpless I am to "do" this thing the right way. It is not like I had imagined. It is much more earthy and grimy.

Michael Card says humility is nothing more than knowing and living the truth,[5] but I thought living the truth would feel different. I expected it to be a sort of Nirvana-like existence. I thought I would be able to see some mission God wanted me to do as if I were a finely tuned spiritual machine that simply needed a directive. Today all I see is a tired, crabby, slightly overweight, middle-aged housewife who spends far too much time playing games on her computer and is numb to what is happening in the world around her. It takes too much energy to see and to care. I don't want to work that hard. So much for a finely tuned machine.

As I deal with the difference between my expectations and the reality of my fast, I realize that one of the goals of fasting is to let go of expectations we have of God and learn to simply listen to Him. Ironic.

*"Incline your ear and come to Me.
Listen, that you may live." (Isaiah 55:3)*

- How are the realities of fasting different from what you expected fasting to be like? What is better than expected? What is harder?

- Read Deuteronomy 8:2. God has a specific purpose for leading us through the wilderness of fasting. What is it?

- What new truths have you already learned about yourself through this discipline?

- Write a letter to God asking Him specific questions about things you need to understand about your spiritual life and your walk with Him. Take some time alone and read this letter back to Him as a prayer.

DAY 16

In one corner of my church's small prayer room, resting on the floor against the wall, is a print of Jesus in a red plastic frame. You have probably seen this image or one much like it. Jesus is laughing in the picture. There isn't much else—just Jesus, with His wavy brown hair and surprisingly Caucasian features, laughing as if one of the apostles (probably Peter) has just done some boneheaded thing that struck Him as funny. I like that picture. The image of Jesus cracking up is rare, and I wonder if He would have enjoyed a joke I told or laughed with me when I did something silly. His sense of humor is gloriously displayed in moments of cosmic creative goofiness (the making of the duck-billed platypus, for instance), but what kinds of jokes would He have told? Knock-knock jokes? Riddles? Would the Almighty Creator of the heavens and the earth have played practical jokes?

My friend Lia and I have some strong opinions about this question.

Everyone should have a friend like Lia. We met on a bus that our church chartered to drive us and about fifty other women to a conference in Minneapolis. I had known Lia only casually before that weekend, and during the conference we barely spoke at all. But for some reason, on the ride home we started to chat, and during the two-hour trip, we jelled. By the time the bus pulled into the church parking lot, we were hunkered down, whispering and giggling like giddy twelve-year-olds. Since then, our friendship has grown only deeper.

Lia and I go to Bible study together. We sit together at church (though our husbands have threatened to split us up if we can't sit still and stop whispering). We take our kids to the beach together. We are the same age, committed many of the same sins, and found sisterhood in salvation. I don't like to revisit my murky past, but with Lia I don't mind so much. We made the same mistakes and have such similar regrets that talking about the past with her gives me perspective.

My daughters and I went to Lia's today. We hung out and watched the latest Teletubbies videos with Lia's little girls, Brexten and Emma, while she ran errands in town. After a couple of hours, she came back carrying a big, greasy bag of fast food. The girls cheered. My stomach responded with a famished lurch. Lia gave me a cautious smile. "I thought this would be easier on you than smelling food cooking." I told her the fast food was a good idea and the smells wouldn't bother me. Normally, they didn't. But as she gathered the girls around the table and started doling out fries and burgers, she pulled one sandwich out of the bag and set it aside for herself. I recognized the grease-spotted, light blue wrapper immediately. I could see the splotches of creamy white tartar sauce squished up against the sides of the wrapper. It was the crème de la crème of fast food. It was a fish fillet sandwich.

I love fish fillet sandwiches. I love the crispy brown breading on the gooey, mushy fish patty topped off with a large dollop of tartar sauce and surrounded by the soft, white, overprocessed bun—it is a nutritional nightmare, a guilty gastric pleasure. A mean thought regarding the fish fillet and the nearby garbage disposal lurked around the protective edges of my mind. My younger daughter seemed to pick up on my state of mind. She slipped from her chair and crossed the kitchen to circle my waist with her small arms in an enthusiastic hug. Her face was flattened against my stomach, and I could feel her little jaw working fries as she clung to me. My other daughter watched from her place at the table, her blue eyes doleful as she nibbled the burger. Liz turned me loose and went back to her spot without a word. I poured myself a glass of juice and slunk off to the living room, feeling starved and pitiful.

I rarely struggle so, but as I curled up on the living room couch and turned my attention to the moronic antics of the brightly colored characters on television, my stomach growled. *Okay, Jesus,* I prayed silently, *this must be one of those pop quizzes. Give me strength not to go and beat Lia up and take her sandwich away. Use this to make me more like You. Help!*

"Oh, man. I can't believe it!" Lia griped from the kitchen. I didn't move since her tone was one of dismay rather than panic. I figured somebody at the table spilled her pop. I waited to hear the sounds of mopping up, but instead Lia came stomping out of the kitchen, holding in one hand the top of her bun, in the other hand the bottom. The bun was smeared with tartar sauce but otherwise empty.

"What's wrong?" I asked.

"They didn't put any fish on my sandwich!"

I looked at her, incredulous. Whoever was in charge of assembling sandwiches at the fast-food restaurant had somehow overlooked the fact that a fish fillet sandwich is supposed to have a fish fillet. As Lia turned around and headed back into the kitchen, I started laughing, and within a few seconds, I was hysterical. I began to howl, curled up on the couch, holding my stomach, laughing with such force that snotty-sounding little snorts escaped from my nose. From the kitchen, the kids started to laugh like kids do when they hear adults make odd bodily noises. Lia started laughing too. I knew without looking at her that she was eating her tartar sauce sandwich.

After the laughter cooled and I was left with little, jerky, slobbering giggles, Lia came back into the room, slurping her soda. "Let me guess," she said, "that you were praying?" All I could do was nod, wiping mascara off of my cheeks. She rolled her eyes, chuckled, and went back into the kitchen to eat her fries. Alone in the living room again, the image of Jesus in the red plastic frame flashed through my mind, and I imagined the deep, clear gales of His laugh echoing through the vaults of heaven.

God has made laughter for me; everyone who hears
will laugh with me. (Genesis 21:6)

- What do you think about Jesus having a sense of humor?

- Write a brief narrative of a time when you think God was laughing with you over events in your life.

- Read Zephaniah 3:17. Ponder the reality of the Lord quieting you with His love and rejoicing over you. Has anyone ever rejoiced over you? How does this verse make you feel about who God is?

DAY 17

I had a call today from someone who wanted to ask some questions about fasting. She wanted to know what I had "seen God do" as a result of engaging in a fast. I started telling her about the way God has used this discipline in my life to help me learn submission and obedience, but she stopped me. She wanted to know specific events that God had brought about because of fasting. I started telling her about the incredible moves of God in our prayer group that have occurred while people were fasting corporately, but she stopped me again. She asked once more, slowly as if she were talking to a very stupid child, if I could tell her of specific, supernatural, unexplainable events that had occurred because I had fasted.

"Oh, I get it. You mean like miracles."

"Yes," she said.

"Signs and wonders?" I asked.

"Exactly," she said.

"Nope," I said. "I won't be able to tell you about a single one." Note that I didn't say those kinds of things had never happened. I said I wouldn't tell her about them.

I believe the attitude that the fast exists as a means to force God's hand to action is ridiculous and incredibly offensive. Human beings need to keep their perspective: We serve

God, not the other way around. We can't possibly put God in a position of being beholden to us. When King David and Bathsheba became the parents of a son conceived as a result of their sin, David was warned by the prophet Nathan that the child was destined to die. David wept and fasted for seven days, but God did not relent, and the child died. David was able to accept God's decision because he understood that God is sovereign. We also do not fast to cause God to perform a miracle, although He sometimes does the impossible in response to the fast. Ultimately, we fast out of obedience.

In Matthew 6, Jesus talked about fasting, praying, and giving at the same time and treated them the same way. Over the years, I have seen amazing moves of God as a result of prayer: diseases cured, cancer removed, prodigal children returned with a passion for the Lord, relationships restored. I have experienced times in prayer that were so powerful that I felt I could reach up and touch the face of God, times when I was an emotional mess and He answered my questions so specifically and tenderly that I wept with gratitude. But that happens only what, maybe a couple times a year? The rest of the time spent in prayer is more like labor: prayers born out of obedience and necessity when I don't see mountains move or kingdoms come. Most of the time, prayer is more utilitarian, and I walk away from the time on my knees thinking, *Well, that needed to be done. What's next on the agenda?*

Giving works the same way. To give in response to a specific calling and see amazing results is joyous, but most of the time,

I drop an envelope into the offering plate out of love and simple obedience and never know how God uses that money. Why should fasting be any different? We don't see every result of our prayers, and we don't see every result of our giving, so why should we insist on seeing every result of our fast? Shouldn't we be obedient and fast because Jesus expects us to and because the experiences of thousands of people before us tell us that this obedience will work godliness in us?

> *Why do you complain against Him*
> *That He does not give an account of all His*
> *   doings?*
> *Indeed God speaks once,*
> *Or twice, yet no one notices it. (Job 33:13-14)*

- Read Matthew 6:1-18. What does God expect from us regarding prayer, fasting, and giving?

- Scripture does not command us to fast on a certain day or for a specific length of time. However, incorporating fasting into your life means making a plan for when you will fast. How often will you fast, and for how long?

- What do you expect God to do in response to your regular fasts?

- How will you feel if He does not respond in the way you have hoped? Will you still consider Him worthy to be praised?

DAY 18

Last night I went to my mother's house for a visit. She made a fantastic meal: roast beef, mashed potatoes, gravy, and steamed carrots. She heaped a plateful for me, seated me at her table, and put the plate in front of me. I had tunneled my way through most of the potatoes and gravy when I suddenly remembered that I was fasting.

I felt a deep sense of panic and despair. My heart started pounding. I felt like crying. I stared down at my half-empty plate, trying to figure out what to do. *Should I just stop eating and resume my fast as if nothing ever happened? Should I consider the fast irrevocably broken and try again next year?* I felt sick. I had failed—not out of rebellion but out of forgetfulness and stupidity.

Then I woke up, my heart pounding and my mouth watering.

Food dreams are one of the most common phenomena of long fasts. I suppose they are the result of a rumbling stomach coming into conflict with a determined spirit.

In one such dream, I found myself wandering along a moonlit boardwalk at a posh resort with a small child in tow. It was a balmy summer night. The kid I was leading by the hand was whining and crying because she was hungry. We trudged all around, turning boardwalks and marching endlessly. Every now and then I would come across another person and ask if he knew where the resort's restaurant was. He would give me directions, and I would follow them, only to end up lost once more. Once or twice I got close enough to the restaurant to find its windows and see people sitting at tables richly spread with heavy white tablecloths and elegant candles, loaded to capacity with sumptuous foods of every description, but I never could find the door to get inside. The child whined on and on. When I woke up, my stomach was gurgling.

Our dreams are so obvious sometimes!

Food dreams can be generated on two different levels: They can simply be the result of the body insisting that you give it what it wants (the flesh does not give up easily, and sleep won't stop the occasional tantrum), or they could be from a latent fear that we will somehow ruin our fast by accident.

I occasionally have similar dreams that I am smoking, even though I quit smoking more than a decade ago. I will never accidentally put a cigarette in my mouth and light it up. Choosing to be a nonsmoker means that I will remain a nonsmoker for the rest of my life, even if someone pins me to the floor and shoves a lit cigarette between my lips. I take responsibility for controlling what I can, and I can control remaining a nonsmoker, just like I can control my eating. The fear of accidentally wrecking a fast is a real one, but unlikely to be realized. Even if you do inadvertently eat something during your fast, it doesn't necessarily mean you've completely ruined it.

My friend Don did have an "accidental eating incident." He was within days of finishing a long fast, and he and his wife were greeters as people made their way into their weekly Sunday school class. Don was chatting with some newcomers when a plate filled with sugar-covered donut holes passed in front of him. Without thinking, he took some of the donut holes and popped one into his mouth. He began to chew while his wife, unwilling to make a scene, watched in horror. After just a few seconds, Don realized his mistake and quickly covered his mouth with a napkin, spewing chewed donut hole out and probably horrifying the new couple standing in front of him. He excused himself and stepped to a trash can to deposit the soggy napkin and the remaining donut holes as his wife stood nearby caught in a fit of laughter no one else quite understood.

Determined as we might be, we are humans and therefore subject to human errors. One of the biggest errors we make is shrugging off our responsibility to take control of what is within our control, and our physical selves are well within our control. The mind sets the limitations for the body, not the other way around. If Jesus had let His physical body decide His destiny, we would be eternally hopeless.

I would have despaired unless I had believed that I would see the goodness of the LORD

In the land of the living.
Wait for the LORD;
Be strong and let your heart take courage;
Yes, wait for the LORD. (Psalm 27:13-14)

- During your fast, what dreams have you had regarding food?

- Read Psalm 103:11-14. According to these verses, what is God's attitude toward us when we make a mistake?

DAY 19

The other day, my friend Sandy asked me about fasting. She feels as though God is trying to lead her toward this discipline, but the moment she tries a short fast, she starts to feel desperate for food. The very idea of fasting makes her feel as though she is starving, which in turn makes her crabby. I told her that I still have that same experience and that I used to blame the crabbiness on being hungry. But there is one thing fasting has taught me very plainly: The irritability I feel during a fast cannot be blamed on hunger.

A fast is like a magnifying glass that focuses on who we are. If I begin a fast and I feel hungry and angry, I know the fast is making me feel hungry but not angry. The fast is not capable of making me angry. The anger was already there, and the fast stripped away my ability to hide it. If I fast and I feel hungry and frustrated, then I know that I am a frustrated person. The fast does not make me frustrated, only hungry.

I can feel hungry without being angry. I can feel hungry without being frustrated. I can feel hungry and rejoice. I can feel hungry and praise God. Paul was under pressure constantly during some of his missionary journeys, but that pressure did not cause him to give up. Instead, he learned how to be abased and how to abound.

The circumstances around me can make it easier to live or they can make it more difficult to live, but they should not have the power to make me a miserable person. If they do, I can be sure I have not yet learned what Jesus meant when He said we were to be in the world but not of it.

A fast shows us the things we have managed to hide from ourselves for years. That is what makes fasting so dangerous: knowledge. The fast is a revealer, and once we know something about ourselves, we cannot unknow it. We have to start making decisions about what we are going to do with that knowledge.

I have learned that I am essentially a lazy person. I will always take the easy way out of things, even if taking the easy way means making things harder for other people. I duck from my responsibilities and let others pick up the slack for me. Now that I know that, I have to deal with it. Furthermore, now that I know that, I see it in myself all the time. I can't escape it. Either I need to accept it and go through the rest of my life with that handicap, or I have to correct the long-standing tendency to be lazy. I am unwilling to live with it. Correcting it is going to take a lot of work.

Fasts can cause emotional turmoil, so it is ironic that fasting actually made its way into biblical history because it was the response people had to times of turmoil. David fasted when his child was dying (see 2 Samuel 12:16). Darius fasted during the night while Daniel was in the lion's den (see Daniel 6:18). Whole nations fasted to show repentance and ask for God's mercy or to show desperation and ask for God's help (see Esther 4:16; Jonah 3:5). The process has a tendency to realign us with our Lord's opinion on a matter, to bring us back to the place where His will is what matters most. Fasting during troubled times—whether physical, spiritual, emotional, or even financial—does not guarantee God will fix our problems. It does, however, help us catch a glimpse of the problem from His point of view. And that can often be enough for us to reconsider how we have been dealing with the problem all along.

That said, I have found that during some struggles, a fast is the last thing I want to engage in. A few years ago, I planned a three-day fast, but the day before it started I got a call telling me that my mom was ill. After driving frantically for three hours to the emergency room and pacing outside a closed white door for a few hours more, I learned that Mom had had a heart attack and needed surgery. Emotionally strung out and huddled together with my sisters in a hospital waiting room, I thought about the fast that I had planned to start in just a few hours. My blood pressure went up. I simply was in no shape to fast. Though I did not have much of an appetite anyway, I needed the freedom to eat if my body called for food. Under the weight of Mom's illness, the additional burden of a fast was more than I could carry. I prayed silently and immediately felt a sense of peace about not fasting.

Fasting takes a tremendous amount of emotional energy. Sometimes during a struggle, it can act as a catalyst for deep prayer and a demonstration of reliance on God. But sometimes during crisis, the fast is a drain on mental and emotional resources a person cannot spare. The key, as always, is prayer. We must seek God for an answer as to whether the fast is appropriate during a struggle.

Search me, O God, and know my heart;
Try me and know my anxious thoughts;
And see if there be any hurtful way in me,
And lead me in the everlasting way.

(Psalm 139:23-24)

• What is the primary negative feeling you notice when you decide you will fast?

• What is the primary negative feeling you notice while fasting?

• What do these feelings reveal to you about your need for spiritual growth?

DAY 20

The halfway mark—yippee!

I am feeling good today. Maybe it's because I stayed up and prayed so long last night. Less hunger, more patience. I keep reminding myself that faithfulness is a choice, not an emotion.

A few months ago, Lia's little girl Emma decided she wanted to fast. Emma is five with a porcelain heart-shaped face, a swirl of soft blonde hair, and eyes the color of burnt honey. She has a tiny baby-doll voice, but she also has unusual wisdom, so we have learned to listen to her when she talks. Rather than discouraging Emma by telling her she is too young to fast, Lia talked to her. "Why," Lia asked, "do you think you should fast?" "Because," Emma wisely replied, "God thinks we should."

How could Lia argue with that?

Lia and Emma sat down and prayed about Emma's desire to fast. Then they talked about what she might give up and for how long. They decided she would give up peanut butter toast for seven days.

Now, Emma loves peanut butter toast. I don't mean she likes it quite a bit—I mean she *loves* peanut butter toast. It is a staple in her young diet. But she felt that would be a good thing to give up because she didn't want to give up anything she would not miss. She instinctively knew sacrifice dictates there is a cost involved.

Emma was excited and wanted to begin her fast right away. Lia, cautious not to let her child make a vow without thinking it through, told her she could begin the next morning if she still felt she was doing the right thing. Emma's resolve remained firm the next day, so her fast began.

Over the next couple of days, Emma's will remained constant. The girl has iron in her spine. If Lia forgot about the fast and offered to make some toast, she would get a staunch reminder. Brexten, who outranks Emma in age by just over a year, encouraged her little sister to stay firm, sometimes forgoing peanut butter toast herself in a show of solidarity. They prayed together, asking God to help Emma know Him better through the toast fast. The day before the fast was to end, Emma hit the first deep struggle of her vow.

Lia's husband, Mark, is an over-the-road truck driver, so he relishes the Sundays he can be home to make the family a big post-church brunch. He made eggs, bacon, sausage, and toast, and after the family had feasted, one lonely piece of peanut butter toast still remained on the edge of his plate. He asked if anyone wanted his last piece of toast.

Emma pushed her plate away, looked up, and began to cry. Across the table, Lia watched Emma's tears plowing wet furrows down her small, cherubic face. *She was so close to being done. Certainly God would understand if Emma broke her fast just one day early? What should a parent do? What would Jesus do?*

Lia stood and scooped Emma from her place at the table, taking her to the living room. She sat in a rocking chair with her child curled in her lap and whispered prayers into her ears until Emma quieted. The temptation had passed. She went back to the table and helped her dad clean up the plates. Lia stayed in the chair, praying.

The next morning, Lia woke early and pulled bread and peanut butter from the cupboard. As soon as Emma woke, Lia hugged her, prayed with her, and served her some warm, fresh peanut butter toast.

Emma had two pieces for breakfast.

She had two more for lunch.

When Lia told me this story, it brought tears to my ears. What a pure sacrifice for a child to give up something she loves, something good and right, in order to pursue God. What a pure picture of the body of Christ for Lia to pick up one who is weak and hold her in comfort and prayer until the danger passes. I could not in my wildest imagination think of a more perfect illustration of the way a fast should be offered by one and upheld by the many.

I will not offer my God that which has cost me nothing. (2 Samuel 24:24, my paraphrase)

- Some people think "Emma's Peanut Butter Fast" is a beautiful story, but others feel that fasting by children is inappropriate. How do you feel about it? Why?

- What is the appropriate age for starting to participate in simple fasts like the one Emma completed? Why?

- How do you define a sacrifice that is pleasing to God? Can a child make such a sacrifice?

DAY 21

I woke in the early morning and stretched, feeling lean and powerful. It was still dark outside. I couldn't resist slipping out from under the covers and stepping to the window. I opened it about six inches, and cold, crisp air rushed in. I quickly climbed back into bed as the cold air hit Tim and he grunted, burrowing under the covers. The air was refreshing, energizing, pure. Tim mumbled something about catching pneumonia and pulled me closer. I was not worried. I had never felt more whole.

God loves physical matter. It was His idea. So was the human body. Bone, muscle, tendon, heart, lung, and blood all come together in a miraculous manner to form that mass of humanity commonly known as Us. My mom worked as a nurse in a newborn nursery, and in all her years of attending deliveries and caring for newborns, she saw very few infants with deformities. Most were perfect—a head, a body, a matching set of ten fingers and toes—and given the chemistry and physiology that has to come together to build the framework for human life, it is nothing short of miraculous that *any* babies come through the process whole and wailing. At birth, most of us were given this gift of strong, working human machinery: a place to be, a vehicle for getting us from where we are to where we are headed, our singular option for residence during our terrestrial stay. Our bodies don't make us human; they make us human beings. Or better said, they make us humans being.

A fast is the right time to contemplate the wonder of humans being. I can appreciate the wondrous ability of the human form more every year, even though nature says I should be declining physically as I age. I gratefully accept whatever freedom and power my physicality can give me because my prior record as a steward of this flesh is poor. It took years for me to break free of the drink/smoke/eat-like-a-pig cycle that I developed early in my youth. I bought into the lie that I had the right to do whatever I wanted with my body and that no one had the right to contradict my desires. That lie says I belong to me.

Eventually, I became a Christian, and soon after, it occurred to me that my body should not make decisions for which my mind would be blamed. Once I realized there needed to be something other than childish impulse and lusty appetite steering the ship, I accepted control of my habits, and things improved. My body became something to value, protect, train, and enjoy. Marriage to a godly man taught me what a source of delight my physical self can be. Childbearing allowed me to see a miracle: a little ball of dust and clay, knit together with DNA from my husband and me in the warp and woof of human fabric to become a whole different someone. But still, the lie that says I can do whatever I want stays with me and continues to pervert my understanding of faith and my place in this sea of humanity. I actively resist that lie with the Word of God, the living Word that tells me I am one part of a complex mystery eternal in scope. I belong to something much higher than little me. All of me, even my physical self, matters in that plan.

You are not your own; you were bought at a price.
(1 Corinthians 6:19-20, NIV)

- Read 1 Corinthians 12:13. If you are not your own but belong to the body of Christ, how does that change your responsibility to care for your physical body?

- Are there areas of your life for which you have avoided assuming responsibility? What are they?

- Are you willing to make a decision to take responsibility for your thoughts and actions? If so, write out a statement of intent to that effect and read it to God as a prayer.

DAY 22

The temperature finally broke loose from the negatives and bounded up to twenty above zero, which was all the excuse I needed to bundle up and go for a long walk. Noise is again a problem for me, and the quiet of a Minnesota winter afternoon was heavenly. The sun tried its best to seep through the clouds, and a steady flurry of fat white flakes floated down through absolute stillness—life in a snow globe. Other than an occasional watery feeling in my leg muscles, I feel strong and light, clean.

Later at home as I put away all of the snow clothes, Liz found me and asked what's for supper. I told her we were having soup broth. She rolled her eyes and went to dig through the freezer for something like a meal. She came back with frozen pork chops, retrieved noodles and a box of corn muffin mix from the pantry, and kissed my cheek on the way out of the kitchen. I started cooking.

Minutes later, I was in trouble. The walk, the fresh air, and the frying chops had my stomach wailing for food. I felt shaky and weak. I got to the pantry, pulled out a can of soup, and struggled to work the can opener with trembling hands. I heated the soup quickly, scooping a few spoonfuls of broth into my mouth from the kettle. I poured the hot broth into a cup, lifted it to my greedy lips, and gulped, burning my mouth.

The nourishment from the soup began to work its magic in seconds. Muscles stopped quivering, and the famished feeling eased. By the time Liz wandered back into the kitchen to ask how soon supper would be ready, the crisis had passed. *Stupid,* I scolded myself. *Such a long walk in cold weather was too much.*

Except for quiet walks, I give up my usual exercise routine during my fast. Giving up workouts is part of the sacrifice that comes along with the vow, and it is no small thing: Muscle tone and endurance that have taken months to build can disappear very quickly during a time of stillness. Here is where counting the cost goes beyond the simple question of whether or not one is willing to give up food for a time.

Of course, not all physical activity can be avoided. Being part of a physical world requires a certain amount of daily activity. Our family used to live on a small horse farm, and the responsibility for feeding the horses in the morning always fell to me. Because chores need doing regardless of fasts, I learned to take my time, carrying one bale of hay at a time instead of two, stopping to rest if I felt weak or dizzy, and using a wheelbarrow more. I have the habit of priding myself on my physical strength, which is not exactly fearsome, but I can hold my own. During a fast, that pride takes a beating. The weight of human weakness, the reality of being made of dust and clay, settles in through the repeated process of needing to slow down, rest often, and accept help.

The amount of physical activity a faster engages in should

be commensurate with the manner and duration of the fast. It is not advisable, or even possible, to maintain a running or weight-training schedule while on an extended fast. For a fast of a single day, nothing more than simple walking is recommended. Embracing weakness is a part of the sacrifice and humility of this discipline.

Being weak means accepting limits to what one can wisely do. The difference between abusive ascetic practice and the godly discipline of fasting is self-preservation. The ascetic wants to look as bad as she feels, wearing physical pain like a mantle, and ramrod her way through a "normal" day despite exhaustion. The ascetic mindset is, *Bring it on, God. You won't wear me down.* The wise faster offers her small sacrifice of abstinence, accepting boundaries and yielding to limitations with humility.

My knees give way from fasting;
my body is thin and gaunt. (Psalm 109:24, NIV)

- Fasting means setting aside physical goals for a period of time. What might you need to give up in order to fast?

- Do you consider yourself someone who rejoices in her physical abilities? If so, how do you feel about losing ground physically during your fast?

- Are the other people in your house willing to take on extra work during your vow? If you ask them for more help, how should you react to their response if it is positive? What if it is negative?

DAY 23

There is a small group of people in my city, maybe twenty of us, who are engaged in fasts of various length and form. We gather about once a week to pray for our city and the churches in our area. These prayer times are open to anyone, so frequently people who are not fasting attend. A couple of days ago we met to pray, and after the prayer time I overheard part of a conversation that made me pause and rethink my reasons for doing this fast at all. Someone asked a woman who is on her own long vow why she was fasting. She responded that she was fasting to prove to God that she loves Him.

That answer felt so wrong. *Is that what I am doing? Am I on this fast so that I can prove something?* I walked away from the conversation deeply provoked. The strong emotion was convicting, as I am provoked only when I fear the presence of an ugly truth. I went out to my car and cranked the engine over, letting it warm as I thought about the "whys" of a long fast.

I spent a few days mulling over this issue as I sipped cups of tea or glasses of vegetable juice, and this is what I have come up with. It seems to me that the notion of "proving" anything to God is based on the assumption that it is possible to hide something from God. Bad assumption. If God searches the heart the way Scripture says He does, then not only does He know exactly how I feel about Him, but He knows how I feel even better than I do. I imagine He can glance down from heaven at any given moment and see how much or how little I love Him, regardless of what I am doing when He looks. So it's ridiculous to think of something—of *anything*—I do becoming proof of devotion to One who can plainly see my heart.

Maybe that woman was thinking of Jesus' repeated statement in John 14–15 that if we love Him, we will obey Him. No point in trying to convince anyone that we love God if we don't bother to obey what He says. Obedience does give other people some sense of how we feel about Him. However, that's about everyday obedience to God's Law, and it doesn't apply to spending forty days on broth and carrot juice. I know I am not doing this to prove anything, so I am left wondering, *Why do I fast?*

I grew up in a household where we "fasted" on Fridays during Lent by avoiding meat. Other people might have caught on to the spiritual implications of that little sacrifice early on, but somehow I equated the Friday "fast" with getting the opportunity to eat seafood at home, a rare treat for us. I missed the point of fasting. Actually, I missed all the points involving faith and salvation until years later.

One cold winter night, at the age of nineteen, I sat in the living room of my tiny college apartment and followed a Baptist preacher of the hellfire-and-brimstone variety to the Cross. I married a year later, and when we had children, I settled into a comfortable rhythm of caring for my family. I read my Bible every day, joined a theologically solid church, prayed, and chronically failed to learn the practical application of faith: consistent obedience to God's Word.

It seemed to me that half the time I was faced with a decision, I did not know the godly thing to do until about five minutes after I had already made the wrong choice. It was as if the Holy Spirit in me was hooked up to a delayed-reaction timer that went off only after I irrevocably goofed up. The other half of the time, I knew what the right choice was but just didn't want to make the right choice. I could find a million good reasons to do what I wanted rather than what God wanted. At that time, simply being obedient wasn't enough for me.

Many years later, God started waking me out of a sound sleep in the middle of the night and nudging me to get up and pray. For several nights, I would patiently explain to God that I was a graduate student and a teacher and a mom of three little kids who needed every available second of slumber I could scrape together. Then I would roll over and pull blankets over my head as a shield against the Voice of the Divine. After a week or so of this, I heard the one thing that finally broke me. It was as if I heard God say, "Are you going to be obedient or not?" He might have been angry, but if He was, He didn't let it show. But His words were so compelling that I had to get up. I remember staggering down the dark hall to the living room and dropping to my knees beside the couch, rubbing sleep from my eyes and flopping the upper part of my body across the broad cushions. I wondered what Tim would think if he woke up in the morning and found me jackknifed across the seat of the couch, snoring. I began to pray in thick, slow phrases—the best I could manage in my semicatatonic state. I know I prayed for a while, but I remember only one part of that prayer time: I remember praying that God would make me more obedient. The next morning, He led me to fast.

I started with fasting one day a week. I found out that obedience is a thoughtful, active choice and that submitting is powerful. I learned that the joy of deferring to another's will is liberating when the Other really understands who I am in the innermost regions of my being.

No spiritual leaders, desert fathers, pastors, mystics, or monks down through the ages have been able to fully understand why abstaining from food for a certain length of time has this effect on the soul. I don't spend much time anymore wondering about why it works. I just know that through the fast, the Holy Spirit shows me where boundaries between me and God are still high and strong. It helps me know where to put my chisel and hammer to work to take those barriers down. It adds strength and power to each blow. It is imperative for people to know that a fast doesn't actually *do*—it just *shows*. I don't know why. And that, I think, is the crux of why I fast. I am sick of stumbling over barriers that keep me from God and cause me to fail to see that right choice before I choose. It is just a tool in the same way my car is a tool. I don't understand how the car works either; I just know it gets me where I need to go.

Why do I fast?

I fast to know God more.

I fast to see what is keeping me from a clearer view of Him.

I fast out of obedience because He expects me to.

I fast to learn obedience as one who needs to know how to submit.

I fast to model obedience so that other people might get a taste of Him.

I fast to worship Him for what is and express my hope for what could be.

That is why I fast.

> *You do not delight in sacrifice, otherwise I would*
> *   give it;*
> *You are not pleased with burnt offering.*
> *The sacrifices of God are a broken spirit;*
> *A broken and contrite heart, O God, You will not*
> *   despise. (Psalm 51:16-17)*

- Do you think fasting helps you "prove" anything to God? Why or why not?

- What led you to fasting as a discipline? What do you hope to gain by it?

- As you grow in the discipline of fasting, how might you challenge yourself more in order to increase your dependence on God? (Note: This does not necessarily mean longer and more difficult fasts.)

DAY 24

The dog is eating well. I have been feeding her the things I wish I could eat. Tonight she had two oatmeal cookies for a bedtime snack, and now she is curled up on the floor sleeping, looking plump and supremely satisfied.

A friend called today to ask a question about fasting. She and her husband were using natural family planning, and she wanted to know whether I thought fasting would change her normal ovulation. I answered with an emphatic yes. I have known fasting to cause many changes in my body, including pushing my monthly cycle back by as much as a week. I told her to be very careful if she did not want to get pregnant right now. She sighed. I have a feeling my good advice might be a bit too late.

I felt tugged all day to get alone and spend some time in prayer. It seemed as though there was something specific I was to be praying for, but I wasn't sure what. I prayed, but nothing dramatic came to mind. I read Scripture, and again, nothing particularly surprising leapt off the page. I spent the rest of the day washing clothes. It's just an ordinary day, comforting in its familiarity, in its unremarkable rhythms. As the day drew down into a quiet night, the kids headed off down the dark halls to their rooms, my husband dozed in his chair, and I curled up with a cup of hot tea and stared out at the night just beyond my window pane. I prayed, but not with words. It was more a feeling of prayer, a sense of reaching up to God with contentment and gratitude. He responded with a warm wave of divine affection, like a holy wink and the brush of a Hand on my cheek. They say one sign that you truly love someone is feeling comfortable being with him or her in silence. Silence fell around me like a warm blanket, and I felt loved.

Teach us to number our days,
That we may present to You a heart of wisdom.
(Psalm 90:12)

- Many of your fasting days will seem ordinary. To what do you attribute this?

- Read 1 Corinthians 15:58. What does it mean to "be stead-fast" (NASB) or "stand firm" (NIV)?

- When is it easier to remain steadfast: in times of struggle and persecution, or in the long, uneventful days of ordinary living? Why?

DAY 25

Tim and I went to a movie tonight. He bought popcorn and candy. I had a bottle of juice and seltzer water in my purse and nursed it through the film. Afterward, we stopped at a restaurant so Tim could get something to eat since he had not eaten supper before the movie. He ordered a plate of pasta, and I was content with a cup of hot chocolate. Understand, I don't mean that I settled for the cocoa; I mean I was truly satisfied with it.

It's funny how little being around food bothers me right now. It's a good thing, because it is impossible to get away from eating in this culture. I never realized how many food commercials there are on television and the radio (usually interspersed with ads for diet pills and health clubs), not to mention the thousands of billboards and newspaper ads. Being almost four weeks into a forty-day fast can give the phrase "all you can eat" a whole new definition.

It must be a protective covering of God's grace that allows me to feel this good. There are times when I will not sit with my family while they eat and even times when Tim notices I am struggling and takes the kids into town to feed them at a fast-food joint. He is great about guarding me that way. But most of the time, I feel content. There are days that I sail through, days when I feel as if I never have to eat again. I have to be careful when I am feeling that strong because I will forget to be mindful of my juice consumption, crashing my blood sugar levels and sending myself into bouts of lightheadedness.

Strangely, I struggle more in a grocery store than in a restaurant. I don't know if it is the variety of food or the sheer volume that makes it hard for me, but I find myself hungry for absolutely everything when I shop. On one grocery-shopping excursion a few years ago, I was so ravenous that I actually bought a can of potted meat. *Potted meat.* In case you don't know what potted meat is, it is a mysterious pink clot of unidentifiable flesh that comes in a tiny blue can with one of those clever metal keys you use to open the lid. It is also one of two things in this world guaranteed to survive a nuclear attack unchanged. The other is the cockroach.

I had no idea what to do with the potted meat. After my fast ended that year, the can of meat was pushed to the very back of my pantry, where it remains to this day. I assume it will still be there in years to come, which will come in handy in the event of a nuclear war.

Countless times during a fast, I have sat with people while they ate, and most of those times the people I was with were not even conscious of the fact that they were eating and I was not. In the event that people suddenly remember that I am fasting, they will usually apologize for eating in front of me (spraying me with little crumbs as they do so) and then pull their plate out of my reach. Apparently, they're concerned I might pounce suddenly and begin stuffing my face with their leftovers.

Of course, I am pretty good to myself. I don't watch the Food Channel. I slip away from the family and take a bath while they are eating. Tim usually oversees kitchen cleanup while I soak in steaming water up to my ears.

I called one friend a few years ago to see how she was doing on her first forty-day fast. It was the last week or so of her vow, and I knew she was having a hard time. When I called, she told me her kids were asleep and she was curled up in bed reading. I asked what she was reading.

"A cookbook," she replied.

"A *cookbook?*" I asked. "Why?"

"I am looking up recipes that I am going to cook once my fast is over," she said.

Oh, mercy.

Maybe the reason I am not bothered more by food is because the war is not for my stomach but for my mind and heart. Fasting is much less a food issue for me than it is an issue of submission. I don't worship food. My god is not a plate of fried potatoes; my god is my desire to be in control of my own destiny, to rule, to decide my fate. So many years after Christ purchased my salvation with His own blood, I want to contest His righteous deed to my soul. I want to be the one who decides for me. I want to rule. This battle is not over what's on the plate; it, like most major battles throughout history, is for a throne.

Is this the kind of fast I have chosen,
only a day for a man to humble himself?
(Isaiah 58:5, NIV)

- Where and when do you struggle the most while fasting?

- Do you have a plan for dealing with these times of temptation?

- What kind of support group do you have? Do you have friends you can call on for encouragement or prayer? If you do not already have people in place to pray for you while you fast, make a list right now of whom you will call for support.

DAY 26

Faster's fog is a term I made up to describe a fuzziness that settles over my mind about halfway through a long fast. I am in the thick of it, meaning I am slow on the uptake right now. I feel slothlike, tranquilized. I could pass a good deal of time staring out a window.

My kids have noticed the stripping of my mental gears, with its grind and jerk, and their reactions are mixed. Bailey and Liz are merciless and tease me about being out to lunch, a favorite metaphor. Joseph has taken his cue from his father and tries to be patient, waiting quietly for me while I flip up couch cushions and dump my purse on yet another quest to relocate my car keys when I swear I just had them in my hand.

That being said, I did have a mildly profound thought today. Perhaps the reason the church in America doesn't fast is because we love food so much or because fasting is hard, but it is equally true that we are ignorant of the reality that Jesus expected His church to engage in this discipline. Many of us grew up in homes where Mom or Dad would say prayers with us as they tucked us in at night, modeling prayer as a routine and important part of our faith. Likewise, we saw Mom or Dad drop one of those funny little white envelopes into our church's offering plate every Sunday. That rubbed off, and America has become the most giving nation in the world. We give and give and give, rebuilding whole nations with our generosity. But did we grow up in homes were we saw people fasting? Did our parents talk to us about the propriety of a regular fast? Did our pastors preach on fasting and let their congregations know it is one of the foundational aspects of normal Christian life? Did we see corporate fasts take place at times of national crisis? I know I didn't. You probably didn't either.

From the Civil War to the mid-1950s, no books were written about fasting. Few churches practiced fasting. We were reacting against the abuse and heresy of the Dark Ages, with its ascetic excess and its perversion of Christian discipline, and some things did not survive the recovery process. The church maintained the importance of prayer despite the fact that Dark Ages–era believers used to beat themselves with short whips while they prayed. We rescued prayer from ascetic aberration, but largely fasting as an appropriate discipline was tossed out with the ascetics' coarse brown cowl and wire undergarments.

To allow a lack of balance in one small parenthesis in history to evolve into permission to avoid a discipline is an epic mistake, and today the church is feeling the loss. We are a people unaccustomed to sacrifice, but things are coming full circle. Fasting is being rediscovered in mainstream Christianity as a valid and valuable response to national crisis. Books are being written. Sermons are being preached. People are nervously entering the wilderness of fasting. It feels weird to them. They think it is somehow irreverent for a form of worship to be so, well, fleshly. They don't know how to react to the physical struggles of fasting. They want to separate the physical and the spiritual, forgetting that the discipline of the physical body is an integral part of spiritual well-being. If it weren't so, God would not equate the physical act of sexual immorality with the spiritual corruption of idolatry (see Colossians 3:5).

God tells us to seek after Him, to search Him out. Seeking and searching are physically active matters, things we do with our bodies as well as with our minds. It was God's idea to create bones, muscle, nerves, and hair. He took mud and made man. We are by nature earthy beings. It's okay for our worship of God (for that is what fasting is) to be physical, empirical, tangible. And it is okay to stumble around a little bit while we learn how to make this discipline work. We are in undiscovered country for our generation.

He shall receive a blessing from the LORD
And righteousness from the God of his salvation.
This is the generation of those who seek Him,
Who seek Your face—even Jacob. (Psalm 24:5-6)

- Have you experienced "faster's fog"? What was it like?

- Was giving of treasure part of your family's regular worship as you were growing up? If not, did anyone model giving for you?

- Was prayer modeled for you as you were growing up? If so, when and how?

- Do you have any childhood memories of people in your body of worship fasting? How did the models, or lack of models, affect your understanding of this discipline?

DAY 27

Tonight I made dinner in the usual rush, galloping into the kitchen a few minutes after five thirty and making my circuit from refrigerator to pantry to cupboards and back to the refrigerator like a pinch hitter rounding bases. I felt good and not hungry, really, except in the I-haven't-eaten-in-twenty-seven-days-and-should-be-hungry sense. I was in a hurry to get supper underway so I could get to my computer and tap out some thoughts on my keyboard while they were still fresh. I extracted some chicken from the back of the freezer, thawed it in the microwave on high heat, and then threw it into a baking pan with rice and some canned soup. I set the timer and gave Liz instructions to put the bread I had let rise all afternoon into the oven in half an hour. Then I disappeared into my office with a cup of hot tea.

I was fine until everything started cooking. Seeing the raw food didn't bother me, but an hour later, I pulled the door to my office open and the smell hit me: chicken and rice and homemade bread. The aroma swaddled me like a warm blanket, and I drifted to the kitchen, my toes scraping the carpet as I floated along. I pulled open the oven door and lifted the plump, lovely loaf of bread out. After tipping it out of its pan to cool for a few minutes, I took out the casserole.

The chicken was perfectly brown, the rice bubbling in gravy.

Tim offered to dish up supper if I wanted to leave. I nodded and headed to the bathroom. I still didn't feel that hungry, but the food smelled good and I wanted it. I squeezed extra toothpaste onto my brush and spent five minutes brushing my teeth, alternately praying for strength and savoring the sounds of glasses clinking and forks scraping. I went back to my office and closed the door firmly, not quite able to shut out the lingering scent of the feast on the table. I slumped into my office chair and stared at my computer screen, pouting. *I want to fast so badly. Where is this resentment coming from? Is it because going without food is hard? Shouldn't that be expected? What does it mean that I feel this way?*

On the corner of my desk was my Bible. I picked it up, opened it at random, and began reading:

> *It is good for me that I was afflicted,*
> *That I may learn Your statutes. (Psalm 119:71)*

It took me a few moments to decide how I felt about that verse. Affliction. Learning. Struggle. Understanding. I flipped through the rest of Psalm 119, and over and over I heard David's heart cry to God: "If you don't save me, no one will. If you don't save me, I shall be utterly destroyed. You are the One in whom I place all of my hope." And something in those phrases hit me in a profound way. David was right. If God does not save me, if He fails me somehow, I *will* be lost. I have not held on to any other safety net. That thought, which would have inspired terror in one less certain about God's ability, gave me tremendous comfort. Again I had to let go of my desire, embrace the struggle, and just let it hurt. I had to let Him do it—let Him work.

Trouble and anguish have come upon me,
Yet Your commandments are my delight.
Your testimonies are righteous forever;
Give me understanding that I may live.
(Psalm 119:143-144)

- How has God used struggle in the past to teach you truths about Himself?

- Why do you think God chooses to use struggle to teach us?

- God loves us so much that He was willing to let His only begotten Son suffer for us. What does it say about Him that He allows us to suffer to learn about Him?

- Think of the times you have had to learn through suffering. Do you believe you could have learned those lessons as well without the pain you endured? If so, how?

DAY 28

I am restless. I woke from a fitful sleep, and the first thing on my mind was money. We are behind on everything, and as I look down the long, dark tunnel of days and bills and paychecks before us, I don't see how we are ever going to catch up. I got out of bed and shuffled to the kitchen. The bright green numbers on the microwave informed me that it was 4:30 a.m.

In the living room, I curled up on the sofa to pray. I suppose I should have gotten on my knees—after all, Jesus prayed on His knees—but I was cold and irritable and hungry, and I didn't really even want to pray. I just wanted to sit there and complain. So that is what I did: I let God have it.

There are things I have to pay—now. The electricity bill is overdue, and there is a bill for fifty dollars at the medical clinic they are threatening to send to collection. I need groceries. I don't know what He expects me to do. *Should I be looking for a different job? Isn't this writing gig His will? Was I wrong? Should I go back to waitressing?*

After unloading about fifteen minutes' worth of whispered rants about lack of money, something tumbled out of my mouth unexpectedly: "I am Your kid," I snapped, "so You have to take care of me."

I thought about that for a moment. I *am* His kid. He does have to take care of me. He took on the responsibility when He adopted me into His family. The idea was a novel one for me, but I found it oddly comforting. I am His problem. So are my bills, my kids, my home, and my job. They're all His problems. If I was wrong about His will and am not supposed to stay home and write, then He needs to tell me that. I know He knows how to communicate. That is His problem too.

The thought tickled at the back of my mind and then cracked open like an egg, its reality trickling through my being. I felt sleepy, so I went back to bed. As the sun struggled to nudge back the thick down of winter darkness, sleep came easily.

I got a call from the insurance company later in the day. Apparently, they should have paid more on a couple of medical bills than they had, so they are sending me a check for two hundred fifty dollars. Then the vet called. I overpaid on my last bill. Should they send a check for one hundred dollars, or would I like to stop and pick it up?

After I hung up the phone, I sat on the couch and stared. I knew I should be thanking Him. I knew I should be thrilled. Instead, I stared stupidly at the floor with my mouth open. His problems indeed.

From days of old they have not heard or perceived
by ear,
Nor has the eye seen a God besides You,
Who acts in behalf of the one who waits for Him.

(Isaiah 64:4)

- Think of a time when God came through for you in a way that was both simple and amazing. Why do you think God moved the way He did?

- Other religious systems find the fact that Christians call God "Father" scandalous. Our identity as children of the Father makes us absolutely unique among the inhabitants of this planet. How would you answer someone who challenged your identity as a child of the living God?

- If God is responsible for your well-being, how does that change the way you look at your daily struggles?

DAY 29

Church was great today. We had Communion. I got to eat one of those crunchy, thin, little Styrofoam wafers that pass for bread. Never mind that it was perfectly tasteless—I got to *chew*.

I grew up Catholic, and we got to take Communion every week. I miss that. We Evangelicals have Communion only a couple of times a month. In the Catholic church, we lined up in the aisles and took turns receiving what the priest called the body and blood of Christ. In the Evangelical church, we sit in the pews, a gold-colored plate is passed to us with the Styrofoam wafers scattered across it, and the pastor instructs us to do this in Jesus' memory. People fight constantly about which is the better way to celebrate Communion. We have gone to war over it. We have burned people at the stake for taking an unpopular stance at the wrong time.

The confusion about how the process should look should not be a surprise. When Jesus sat along the shores of Galilee talking about people eating His flesh and drinking His blood, His own followers were confused. Jesus told them that anyone who did not eat His flesh or drink His blood did not belong to Him. The crowd that was there stirred uncomfortably. They grumbled among themselves that this teaching was, well, new, to say the least.

Some commentators claim Jesus' followers thought He was talking about cannibalism and that was the reason they were outraged. I don't believe it. The Jews who heard Him knew He was talking not about cannibalism but about something far more dangerous: identity.

Jewish law abounds with dietary regulations about what Jews can and cannot eat. Cows and sheep and goats are in; pigs and clams and predatory birds are out. Locusts are in; spiders, thankfully, are out. There are foods that are clean and those that are filthy—no in-between. To eat clean foods makes us clean, but to dare eat unclean foods makes us unworthy to be called sons and daughters of Abraham. Jews believed we are what we eat eons before the health-food industry came up with that clever little slogan. Because of their laws, it was easy to figure out who was a Jew in a mixed crowd. The Jew would be the guy loading up on veal and passing on the pork rinds. Food was more than nutrition; it told the world who you were and whose you were. Identity.

When Jesus said that only those who eat His flesh and drink His blood will belong to Him (see John 6:53-58), He was talking about people submitting to a level of identity far beyond religious tradition. He was talking about a level of intimacy closer than sexual contact. He was talking about actually becoming something new, a being with cells and muscles and neurons powered by the life force of who He is. He was talking about becoming the power and energy behind every beat of our hearts. He meant that unless we let Him live through our bodies, we cannot belong to Him.

The Jews who heard Jesus speak about this were not kidding when they said it was a "hard teaching" (John 6:60, NIV). There was no way to dodge what Jesus demanded or what He was claiming to be. Not all of the Jews understood, but many of those who did understand walked away that day (see John 6:66). Jesus watched them go. Then He turned and asked His disciples if they wanted to go too. They, who had already abandoned every semblance of a normal life to follow Him, gave the only answer they could: "Lord, to whom shall we go? You have words of eternal life" (John 6:68).

"Just as the living Father sent me and I live because of the Father, so the one who feeds on me will live because of me." (John 6:57, NIV)

- What did you grow up believing about the nature of Communion? What do you believe about it today?

- The main point of Communion is to live a life that allows Jesus Christ to live through us. How can we live "communion table" mindsets in our daily lives?

- Read John 6:53-68. Do you agree with Peter's response to Jesus when Jesus asked if he and the others would depart? Why or why not?

DAY 30

A bad day. I woke up late, my arms and legs heavy with aches. I pulled myself upright and sat at the edge of the bed, eyes sticky with sleep and refusing to open. If everyone would have left me alone, I could have slept just like that, hunched over the edge of the bed, feet dangling. Liz banged on my door to tell me we had to leave in ten minutes or she would be late for school. I glanced at the clock and did some quick math, realizing it would be at least fourteen hours before I could sleep again. Depressed, I staggered to the bathroom and splashed cold water on my face until my cheeks went numb. Then I stood stooped over the sink, letting the drips collect into rivulets and flow from my pale face back into the sink and away.

Lately, I can't get enough sleep. I am famished all day long, and no amount of broth or juice satisfies me. I have chronic chills. Diarrhea is an issue. I am crabby with the kids and with Tim and am getting crabbier. This discipline seems so completely useless—I am useless. Somewhere in the upper atmosphere of my brain, where the air is clearer, I recognize those lies, but I was not living from the upper atmosphere today. Today I was in the polluted nether regions of thought and feeling, and lies were the air I breathed when I was there.

I dragged myself through the day, entertaining little fantasies about falling into a coma and waking up when the fast is over. The day wore on and I labored over small tasks to keep myself busy, but I managed to accomplish next to nothing. Tim came home from work and threw me worried glances and then finally ordered me to the bathtub while he fed the kids. The hot bath was an oasis, and I realized I had been chilled all day. Tim came into the bathroom while the kids were cleaning the kitchen and asked me if I was doing all right. I did my best to convince him that I was okay. I hate the fast right now. Despite the struggle, I feel there is something here that God wants me to see, and I do not want to miss what He has for me.

When everyone else went to bed, I stayed up to pray. I needed to know why my fast is so hard if it was His will for me to enter this vow. *Did He really choose this for me, or did I make a mistake? And if I did make a mistake, can I quit? What about the vow I made? Others know about this vow—how would it affect their faith if I gave up? What would that say to my children? Why is my desire to finish this fast at an all-time low?*

Alone in my living room, the weak light from a solitary lamp the only thing between me and complete darkness, I got down on my knees and started pelting God with complaints. I feel sick, frustrated, impatient. Instead of gaining anything spiritually, all I see is utter lack. I feel as though I am fasting for nothing, that there is no reason behind what I am doing. Worst of all, I am scared to death at the prospect of more days like this one. I can't feel this way for ten more days—it's impossible to conceive how God would get glory out of that. I don't know what I can do to turn things around. *Is this what fasting is all about?*

For a while I kept my eyes closed, kneeling on the carpet in front of the couch with a blanket slung over my shoulders and my bare feet poking out from my worn flannel pajamas. I prayed as fervently as I know how. Head bowed, eyes squeezed shut, hands clamped together in preparation for a divine wrestling match, I pureed together complaints and petitions in a living stream of words and phrases that would not make sense to anyone but the Holy Spirit. I fully expected God to show up and reckon with me, to cause me to understand what the vow and that miserable day had to do with His glory. But I was disappointed. He didn't show up in some mystical cloud of Shekinah glory. He didn't even show up as a still, small voice. I was undeniably alone in that room.

Eventually, I ran out of words to pray. I opened my eyes and unclasped my hands, wiggling stiff fingers to encourage blood to revisit my fingertips. The room was steeped in thick darkness, held at bay by the dull yellow light next to me. In the corner of the room was a picture of Tim and me that was taken at a friend's wedding the year before. We are both dressed in wedding finery and smiling broadly at the camera, arms encircling one another. We look every bit the happy couple. How ironic it is to see that picture and know what an illusion those two people were capable of creating. That photo was snapped at one of the worst times in our marriage. We had found ourselves facing a hurricane, unsure whether we had been building our marriage on a foundation that could outlast the wind and tides threatening to destroy it. It was a time to find out whether we had built on sand or stone.

I had been so frightened that I'd asked Tim if he would go to a marriage counselor with me. He was so frightened he said yes. His agreement to seek help told me I was not exaggerating how bad things between us had become. We started to see a counselor and separate the reality of our lives together from idealistic fantasy. We fought and argued and cried—he out of fear and I out of anger that he was fearful. I wanted one of us to have the good sense to maintain the lies that everything would somehow work out fine. His inability to maintain that façade told me we were going down.

Somewhere in all the panic, a new idea emerged and began to take form in my mind. For the first time since we got married, I realized I had a choice about whether or not I wanted to be married to Tim. That choice had always existed, but I had never felt it before. I had always believed married was married, end of story. Finally I realized "not married" was an option—no, more like a threat, a specter of marital annihilation that loomed at the edges of our struggle to survive as a couple. I felt as though I was pinwheeling out over the edge of a canyon. I had to choose Tim or choose something else—there was no in-between—and I felt like leaving.

I have a vivid recollection of a single, victorious moment in that valley of decision. I looked Tim in the eyes and, for the first time since our wedding day, declared my choice: "I choose you," I said. "Every day, no matter how I feel, I will choose you."

The memory of what caused me to choose him is long gone. I don't remember what finally clicked into place for me. But I do remember that the look on his face told me that the depth of his longing to hear those words ran to his very soul.

Since then, our marriage has become something more real than I could have hoped for. It isn't perfect, so I don't let my guard down. I still choose him. The decision to stay married is no longer a settled issue in my mind—it is an ongoing decision. Not choosing is to choose not to stay.

Something in the memory suddenly illuminated the struggle I was feeling tonight. I realized that my problem is not the fast but how I feel about it. My emotions—not the reality of the commitment I made—are driving the fast. The choice to engage in my fast so many days ago is not enough to keep me committed to it; the choice has to be made again. Just like my marriage is a settled issue but my commitment to my marriage could waver, my salvation is a settled matter but my commitment to seek God wavers every day. If I lose the commitment, I don't lose the salvation, but I lose the intimacy that is salvation's greatest reward.

Still kneeling on the living room floor, I folded my hands, closed my eyes, and told my Father the words I realized He longs to hear from me: "I choose You," I whispered. "No matter how I feel, every single day I choose You."

As the bridegroom rejoices over the bride,
So your God will rejoice over you. (Isaiah 62:5)

- What are the biggest choices you have had to make in your life?

- Did you make these choices once, or do they involve ongoing decisions?

- One line in the entry for this day reads, "Not choosing is to choose not to stay." What does that mean to you? How might that statement apply to your choosing or not choosing Christ as your Savior?

DAY 31

Every day the juices and broths can do less to help me regain a feeling of solidness. I never realized to what extent solid food made me feel solid. Living on liquids makes me feel vaporous, insubstantial.

I think about Jesus alone in the desert (see Luke 4:1-2). He must have been terribly weak by this point, without the comfort of even a warm cup of cocoa. He must have been cold, especially at night, if my chills are any indication. Did He have headaches, dizzy spells, and quivering muscles? Did His stomach cramp? Did He know exactly how long He would be fasting, or did He just wait for the Holy Spirit to tell Him when to stop? I wonder if He ever lost track of the number of days He had been fasting or if he prayed fervently that the time of preparation would come to an end.

I think of Paul trekking across Europe, Asia, and the Middle East, often without a meal or a bed (see 2 Corinthians 11:24-27). I think of a million believers in Somalia and North Korea and Vietnam who accept poverty as part of the price they pay for being faithful to the name of Jesus Christ while their governments hate them for it. I think of millions in India who are trapped in the caste system with no hope for this life or the next. I think of missionaries scattered too thin across the globe, eating whatever

God provides and sleeping wherever He allows in a desperate effort to bring life-giving words to those so trapped.

During the year, and during the Lenten season specifically, thousands of people across the globe are fasting. No matter whether or not you know someone else who is fasting, you are never really alone in that wilderness; God may be calling you into a time of deep fellowship with only Him. If you know others who are fasting at the same time, take comfort in the shared journey. Either way, it is a small fellowship of those who feel true hunger and let it act as a catalyst for action, a seedbed for hope, and who don't pretend to understand God's economy but know that sacrifice has value there.

May my prayer be counted as incense before You;
The lifting up of my hands as the evening offering. (Psalm 141:2)

- Think of what Jesus must have experienced in the desert as He passed days and nights alone in the wild. Why do you think the Holy Spirit led Him into this time of fasting? What does it mean to you personally that He completed the fast?

- Have you ever been truly hungry and unable to get to food? (Do not count times of deliberate abstaining from food but rather a time when events conspired against you and you could not eat.) If so, what was that like?

- If you have never experienced such a time of hunger, you are part of a tiny minority on the globe. How does that make you feel?

DAY 32

After my family left to start their day, I settled in for an extended time in prayer. I knelt in my usual spot on the living room floor, but within a few minutes I felt uncomfortable, so I decided to stand and pace around as I prayed. Soon I realized I was doing laps around the coffee table thinking aimless, random thoughts that had nothing to do with prayer. I sat down on the couch and tried for a third time to focus on the Lord, but after a minute or so, I was just staring blankly out the window at the gray snow that has filled my front yard. I sighed and gave up, deciding to play some loud worship music and resume prayer later.

My prayer life is such a roller coaster during a fast. Some days I feel as if I could spend the whole day on my knees; other days I am lucky if I remember to mutter a few drive-by prayers as I race through another twenty-four hours of life. Christians are quick to blame the Devil for unsuccessful prayer times, but he is getting too much credit. Most days, he probably glances at me and knows he doesn't need to waste his time: I am sufficiently distracted by my own life that I am not much of a threat.

But there are days—oh, glorious, lovely days—when prayer flows like a river and I feel as though God is in the room with me, listening to my every word, communing with me, and directing my requests. And those days do seem far more frequent during a time of extended fasting. God is always with believers through the presence of the Holy Spirit, but we are normally not aware of Him. The spiritual insights and sensitivity that fasting affords do not make God draw closer, but they make me more aware of His presence.

> *Those who look to him are radiant;*
> *their faces are never covered with shame.*
> *(Psalm 34:5, NIV)*

- Describe one of your most powerful prayer times. What did it feel like?

- Read Revelation 5:8. Were you aware that the prayers of believers are kept in heaven? How does that change the way you look at prayer?

- What is your usual response when prayer is a struggle for you? How might that be different during times you are fasting?

DAY 33

My husband should be beatified. For all of my nonliturgical friends, what I mean is he should be nominated for sainthood: Saint Tim, patron saint of Men with High Maintenance Wives. He should become a saint because he allows me to fast over and over despite the fact that I am not exactly at my best after a couple of weeks without solid foods. My vow actually creates more work for him, though I strive to keep that from being the case. Like it or not, he goes into the wilderness with me when I fast. That's the hard truth about being one flesh.

My children have grown up hearing the discipline of fasting discussed as a normal part of devotional Christian living, so they do not find the idea odd. On occasion, they decide to fast, but for their own reasons. Tim and I help them decide what kind of fast they should do. A daylight fast, in which they do not eat solid food while the sun is up, is a frequent choice. They have a better understanding of fasting than most adults do.

The support of my family is the undergirding of this fast. I know of a few women who are mocked in their own homes for fasting, and I do not know how they manage. Some women find that getting their spouse's permission to fast is easy, but support for what the fast costs them in terms of a lack of energy and the greater need for physical and emotional aid is nonexistent. I do not advise women in unsympathetic families to engage in a long-term fast unless they have a very high degree of spiritual maturity. The Bible never demands those of us living in the freedom of grace to fast, and Jesus never told us how long or how often we should observe the vow. Fasting one day a week has grown out of tradition, not Scripture. If a woman desires to fast for a long period of time and her family opposes her, she should pray the Lord would work on their hearts; then she should engage in shorter fasts until He does.

If Tim were to grow weary of my fasting and request that I quit, I would do so. He knows how important fasting is to me, and I trust he wouldn't make such a demand of me unless he truly thought I was doing harm to myself, our marriage, or our family. The apostle Paul told the Corinthians that husbands and wives have authority over each others' bodies (see 1 Corinthians 7:4); therefore, I'd willingly submit to my husband's wisdom in this area, even though I'd be disappointed. Of course, we'd have to discuss future fasts and come to an agreement about whether or not I should undertake them.

*Unless the L*ORD *builds the house,*
They labor in vain who build it. (Psalm 127:1)

- Do you have the support of your immediate family as you begin to fast as part of your spiritual growth?

- If so, how do you express your gratitude to them?

- If not, do you understand why they feel they cannot support you? How might your actions and patient responses eventually gain their support?

DAY 34

It's amazing that I can feel so good and look so crummy. The healthy glow of the last two weeks has morphed into a thin and homely stage. My skin looks papery, my complexion pallid. My hair is in complete rebellion, and I have taken to wearing a baseball cap. The overall effect is that I look like a pale, thin, reheated corpse in a hat. The long Minnesota winter, with its endless dull gray skies and frigid temperatures, usually causes me to fade to the shade of a fish's underbelly anyway, but fasting does not help.

A number of people know about my fast and are watching me closely to see how my body will handle the stress. I started praying that God would not allow people to conclude that accepting His invitation to fast is making me sick. I don't want to make a mockery of this discipline by allowing the way I look to confirm in the minds of people that I am crazy or God is mean. I am privileged, and God is incredible beyond my poor ability to say.

Besides, I feel good. I feel light and joyous, and that seems to overflow. Hopefully, that's what people are noticing. The superficial things that normally irritate me just don't seem very important now. Little else besides God's glory seems important. I find delight in making a meal for my family because God delights in a woman who cares for the people He entrusted to her. The meal will not benefit me except in that it pleases God, and that is enough for me.

According to Isaiah 58, the fast that God chooses is not about trapping people into performing a spiritual rite; it is about freedom—freedom from those things that bind us in our everyday lives, from oppression and hopelessness and empty religious ceremony. The freedom He gives is light and life and liberty. The command is to fast from evil before we fast from food—to practice righteousness in all our doings with coworkers, the needy, and our families.

God is not going to bless the evil person with spiritual satisfaction. Isaiah reminds us that we must first take an inventory of our lives to look for obvious sin and then deal with those issues. Then we are in the right position to fast. The promise is that when you fast rightly, "Your light will break forth like the dawn . . . and the glory of the Lord will be your rear guard" (Isaiah 58:8, NIV). No amount of fasting can atone for an evil life.

"Is not this the kind of fasting I have chosen:
to loose the chains of injustice
*   and untie the cords of the yoke,*
to set the oppressed free
*   and break every yoke?*

Is it not to share your food with the hungry
    and to provide the poor wanderer with shelter—
when you see the naked, to clothe him,
    and not to turn away from your own flesh and
    blood?" (Isaiah 58:6-7, NIV)

- Read Matthew 6:17-18. What did Jesus say regarding grooming and the faster?

- How will you handle questions regarding changes in your looks during times of an extended vow?

- How do you think a person's attitude about fasting affects her physical appearance?

DAY 35

I am ready for this fast to be over now. I have less than a week left, and I want to be done. I remember hearing that when a person does a long fast, the grace period in the middle of the fast is followed by true, deep hunger. I am at that point. This whole discipline has lost its charm, and I want out now.

I feel a tug-of-war inside. I wonder what it means that I want out so badly. I can't imagine actually walking to the refrigerator, taking out a storage container, and eating whatever is inside. But I can't really imagine five more days of this hollowness either. It's not that I want to break my fast; it's that I want these last few days to fly by and be over. I wish I could just become unconscious and wake up five days from now.

I keep reminding myself that I can quit if I want to. This fast is not a commandment; it is a grace. If I quit today, Jesus would love me just as much as He would if I finished. *So*, I ask myself, *what is keeping me on the fast?*

I tell myself to calm down. I take my emotions in hand and choose—literally make a conscious choice once again—to continue the fast. I spend some time in prayer and ask Jesus to help me offer the struggle up as a love offering. He does. I know that the battle is in my head and I need to keep a tight rein on my thought life. Jesus knows all about that. He can use the struggle to polish me the same way sand polishes stones on a beach by continuous pounding of the waves.

I said I would do forty days. I feel compelled to keep my word, not because I think it will cause Jesus to love me more but because He already loves me perfectly. It seems there is so little I can do to reflect that love back to Him. I don't want this fast to be a chore; I want it to be a love offering. I wish I didn't feel so frustrated about it. I wish I didn't hate it right now. But those are just feelings, and feelings, I know, are a very poor barometer of what is true.

What I need to remember is, I committed to forty days, not forty *easy* days.

Though He slay me,
I will hope in Him. (Job 13:15)

- What does your response to the fast teach you about your typical response to other times of struggle? How do you want to pray in response to that knowledge?

- How important are your feelings and emotions when it comes to making decisions about how you are going to live? Do you find that your emotions are honest indicators of what is right and true?

- What is the value of committing to a goal? Is the strength of that commitment enough to get you through the struggle of attaining it?

DAY 36

Tonight I made an excuse to go to the store, as the usual nighttime pandemonium with the kids and the television and the ringing phone was driving me nuts. Tim offered to go for me, but I told him I wanted the time alone. I drove slowly, listening to my stomach make occasional rumbling noises, and enjoyed a long wallow in self-pity. I decided to unload my frustrations on God (and called it "prayer" lest a lightning bolt descend from the sky and pierceth my whining hide). I was so sick of my own lament that I gave up and popped a tape into the cassette player to drown out the sound of my voice. It was then that I heard music playing.

Well, yes, you are thinking, *if you popped a tape into the deck, wouldn't you expect to hear music playing?* But I didn't just hear the music, I *heard* the music. Anyone who has ever studied Scripture in a time of great need will know what I mean. I heard it the way that you *see* Scripture when God shines a spotlight on a verse that deals directly with the issue you are facing. It was as if God suddenly "turned up" the volume of the car stereo and I heard these words from the hymn "How Firm a Foundation":[6]

> *When through fiery trials thy pathways shall lie,*
> *My grace, all sufficient, shall be thy supply;*

The flame shall not hurt thee; I only design
Thy dross to consume, and thy gold to refine.

Suddenly I was reeling backward through time and space, back to a night about a year earlier when I was nearing the end of a previous fast. I had been driving to town on some weak excuse just to get away from home and was feeling sad and hungry and frustrated. I popped a tape into the deck to distract myself, and what did I hear playing? Exactly the same singer, same song, same verse: "Thy dross to consume and thy gold to refine."

The skeptics who read this are going to chuckle and shake their heads at my naïveté in believing that hearing the same song on both nights was anything more than a coincidence. That's fine—skeptics of Jesus' day heard God speak and said it was only thunder. I'm not talking about mountains being moved or seas being parted; I'm just talking about God caring a great deal about how I am doing on this fast. I'm talking about God listening to my complaints and patiently reminding me that the struggle is not without gain. I am talking about a God who loves and understands slow learners. I am talking about intimate, one-on-one communication with the One who created everything I see and knows me better than anyone.

And if that's not a miracle, what is?

"Believe Me that I am in the Father and the Father is in Me; otherwise believe because of the works themselves." (John 14:11)

- Do you believe that God cares for every detail of your life? Why or why not?

- When God intervenes in the course of your life, do you consider that a miracle? Why or why not?

- Think of a time when God used a song, Bible verse, timely phone call from a friend, or similar event to reach out to you. How did you react?

DAY 37

My friend Julie really wants to fast, but she can't. It's not that she's sick or her husband has forbidden her from fasting. On the contrary, she is a healthy, vibrant, lovely Christian woman who wants nothing more than to serve and please her Lord. Julie understands fasting, but the problem with her participating in it is that she has a past history of anorexia.

The question of whether people with eating disorders should fast is far too broad to be answered with a simple yes or no. There are too many variables: the type and extent of the disorder, how far back in the person's history the food-related issues go, and the current state of emotional and spiritual maturity. Eating disorders are generally not about food, per se, but about the individual's struggle to control her life. Someone who has grown to trust Christ deeply and can release the desire for control to Him *might* benefit from the discipline, but much would depend on that person's ability to be completely honest about her motives for fasting. It seems foolish and risky to meddle with the recovery of a person with eating disorders by encouraging her to embark on a liquids-only fast.

We need to remember fasting is not about the fast; it's about obedience. The act of going without food is, in itself, spiritually neutral. Eating or not eating is not the point. Nowhere in Scripture did God directly command mankind to observe a fast. There is a command by God to the Jewish nation that they "afflict [their] souls" on the Day of Atonement (see Leviticus 23:27, NKJV), and the word *affliction* (*ânâh* in Hebrew) means "to make oneself weak." Because one symptom of an afflicted soul is a loss of appetite, the act of fasting quickly became synonymous with afflicting the soul. However, the law regarding the Day of Atonement does not directly say to fast.[7]

Fasting is not evidence of piety but a means to it. The purpose of fasting is to create humility of spirit in those who serve God. It makes us soft and elastic, quiet and pliable to the will of Christ, and therefore more available to His purposes. When fasting becomes proof of piety rather than a means to it, the result is spiritual pride and rigidity. The person becomes satisfied with her own "holiness" and no longer hungry for the holiness of God. It is people in that tragic spiritual state that the Father addresses in Isaiah 58 when He says:

> *"Behold, on the day of your fast you find your*
> *   desire,*
> *And drive hard all your workers.*
> *Behold, you fast for contention and strife and to*
> *   strike with a wicked fist." (Isaiah 58:3-4)*

Like prayer and giving, fasting is a means of liberation, setting us free by teaching us the truth of who we are. This type of knowledge must precede liberation, as Jesus pointed out when He said, "You will know the truth, and the truth will set you free."

Some people can't fast. Maybe it is because they are ill, pregnant, or nursing. Maybe it is because they know their fast would be an act of self-worship rather than worship of God. Remember that a fast is not about the fast; it's about obedience. If a person honestly cannot fast, then she needs to pray God will use other tools to teach her how to lean on Him. He will. He lives, and died, for exactly that purpose.

The afflicted will eat and be satisfied;
Those who seek Him will praise the Lord.
Let your heart live forever! (Psalm 22:26)

- Do you have a past history with eating disorders? If so, write out a short summary of your problem.

- If someone with an eating disorder asked you about fasting, how would you respond?

DAY 38

One of my first thoughts upon waking was that I have only two days left of my vow. Mixed emotions followed in the wake of that thought: relief that the struggle will soon be over and sadness that this time set aside for communing with God will end also. That feeling of being set apart has become precious.

I meandered through the morning, grateful for the quiet after the house emptied out. I wandered through rooms, composing a mental list of chores I should complete, and then made the decision to toss the list and have another cup of tea. The house was silent. I curled up with my Bible and opened it to the concordance in the back. That idea of having time "set aside" wouldn't leave me, and I wanted to check something. In the concordance, I found what I was looking for: a hand-scribbled note from some past sermon. It reads, "*palah* = set apart = holiness."

The Hebrew word *palah* is used in Scripture to denote something that has been set apart for use by God. It contains the same idea as the word *holy*. The things used in worship in the old temple system were holy because they were dedicated solely for temple use. Certain days throughout the church calendar are holy because they are devoted to worship of God. God's people are holy because they are separated from the rest of the world by the power of the blood of Christ. What makes something holy, then, is not about performance but about its position as something set apart. By this definition, the fast is holy not because of the length of time I fasted or what I did or didn't drink. The function of the fast is what makes it holy: the act of devoted, dedicated time set aside.

I closed my Bible and turned to face the window. The pale blue sky was hazy with moisture hanging in the air. A few birds, sturdy sparrows, landed in the snow at the edge of the driveway and searched for sustenance. Spring wants to start.

Two days. So many times over the last six weeks I did not think I would make it to this point. Yet here I am, so close to the fortieth day that I can just let the momentum of the weeks behind me sail me forward over the finish line.

> You are A CHOSEN RACE, a royal PRIESTHOOD, A HOLY NATION, A PEOPLE FOR God's OWN POSSESSION, so that you may proclaim the excellencies of Him who has called you out of darkness into His marvelous light. (1 Peter 2:9)

- What does the word *holy* mean to you? It is possible that something can be imperfect but still holy?

- As this time of fasting draws to a close for you, how do you feel? What emotions are most prominent? Which are most surprising?

- How can you take the sense of being set apart into your everyday life?

DAY 39

This morning I was looking for a book in my office and came across a journal I had written in several years ago. I opened it randomly and started reading. Soon I was leafing through the handwritten pages, the book I had been seeking utterly forgotten.

I have to laugh at myself, but the humor is not without pain. There are so many prayers in that journal that were miles off base from what God wanted to do. Over and over I read declarations of faith about what I was sure God was going to do for me, and almost none of them came to pass. There are passages about my longing for more children—something that would be biologically, well, difficult for us but that I begged God to give me anyway. He didn't, or at least He hasn't, and I must say that at this point in my life, God's answering that old prayer would seem like a bad joke. There are other passages: ones about a house I was sure God was going to let us buy (He didn't), people I was sure He wanted me to lead (nope), and ministries I thought I was supposed to start (wrong again). It is a very long written record of misunderstanding and rash misinterpretation of God's plans.

There is so much of *me* in that old journal—pages and pages about what I thought I knew, what I was sure God was telling me. It all sounds incredibly arrogant now, and I have to wonder, *Do I still sound that way?*

There is one other thing I notice in that journal and that's how often God did speak to me. There are little quips about the perfect Scripture given at just the right time, phone calls I received when I was deeply discouraged, money that arrived in time to save us from economic disaster—little lights that told me God was listening nearby. Wrong as I often was, I was never left alone to stumble on without a trail littered with bread crumbs to lead me. My world was too full of me, and He might have been crowded out. Yet He found just enough room, even though my boast took up so much space. He met me despite me.

I want to be free of me, of my demands and expectations and the hoops I try to get God to jump through. His love abounds even when I am so full of myself that I can barely see Him, but I want to see Him more.

I feel foolish. The temptation to take the journal and burn it before anyone else happens to pick it up is so strong, but I know I can't—I must not. The journal was meant to be a testimony to the world about the faithfulness of God, but it has become a letter to myself. I need to reread this letter and remind myself of where I have been. Keeping such a record and heeding its lessons is the only guarantee that I will not have to come back this way again.

Do not remember the sins of my youth or my
transgressions;
According to Your lovingkindness remember me,
For Your goodness' sake, O LORD. (Psalm 25:7)

- What mistakes have you made in your past that embarrass or haunt you now? Have you confessed those sins?

- What mistakes have you made in understanding God's will for you? Have you ever felt sure you "heard" God tell you something, only to realize later you were wrong?

- Does fasting help you see clearly where you have made mistakes in the past? If so, how?

DAY 40

11:22 p.m.

I am sitting alone in my office in a silence broken by only the occasional gust of wind against the side of the house. In just under forty minutes, my fast will officially end.

I debated about whether or not I should stay awake until midnight and eat something then. Tim offered to stay up with me and take me to an all-night restaurant for a literal "break-fast." I loved the sentiment, but what I really wanted was to spend the last few hours of my fast alone. Seeing this fast end is a joy but not without loss. Although I cannot honestly say I have felt God's presence constantly throughout the last six weeks, I can say I have felt as though He has been *intent* on me. It feels as if He has watched me more closely than He usually does, but it's more likely that I have simply seen more clearly how intent He has always been on me.

I feel starved. Health-food gurus encourage fasters to break their fast with fresh fruits and vegetables, and I agree it's a very good idea; however, I think I'll make myself a hot dog and grab some cheese curls to go with it. I'll wash it down with some water. No juice for me, thank you. I might get a stomachache, but I'll live.

As I sit here in the quiet, my Bible read-through has me in the closing chapters of John's gospel. I did not plan that; it just turned out that way. Jesus' plea to Peter that the willful disciple feed His lambs echoes in my mind (see John 21:15). I want to bring more of Jesus to people, yet I can't go to others and tell them what I haven't up to this point lived. I have been expecting God to use this fast to equip me for ministry, but He is equipping me just to live in a more steadfast way. I need to live *Him* more and show them what He looks like that way.

I feel a deep sense of gratitude for the privilege of going through this fast. I can let go of the weight of this vow, knowing it is successfully done. I did not fast perfectly, but I have long since given up the notion that I can do anything perfectly.

I have been faithful.

My spirit is quiet, serene.

It feels like coming home. It feels like entering a room of soft yellow light, closing the door against the darkness, and laying aside the burden I have been carrying. It is like slipping into the comfort of home and finding well-deserved rest in a very good place.

"Go home to your people and report to them what great things the Lord has done for you, and how He had mercy on you." (Mark 5:19)

- Successfully completing a fast of any length is a joy. Write a letter to Jesus describing your thoughts and feelings on having completed your time of fasting. Write down what you think He wanted you to learn in the process of fasting and what you hope to do with that new knowledge.

APPENDIX A

TIPS FOR A SUCCESSFUL FAST

- Before beginning a fast, seek advice from a physician familiar with fasting.
- Decide what kind of vow and how long your vow will last *before* the onset of the fast. Remember, your heart attitude about your fast is far more important than the length of time or the type of fast you enter. Write down what you plan to ingest, how long the fast will last, and what you intend to pray about during that time.
- If you are new to this discipline, try starting with a daylight fast. From dawn to sunset, abstain from solid food, choosing fresh vegetable and fruit juices. Extend the time of the fast as you begin to understand the discipline. Remember that the difficulty of the fast is not important, but make a pure, honest assessment of what your fast should include.
- Remember to drink plenty of water.
- Taking vitamins is a good idea and can help your body cope with the stress of going without solid food.
- Expect fasting to be hard. Accept the reality that physical disciplines are physically challenging.
- Protect yourself from negative spiritual and emotional influences during your vow. Fasting creates spiritual

tenderness, so be mindful of what images, programs, or movies you watch.

- Pray as much as possible during the fast.
- Do not be surprised by negative emotions. When they come, ask God to show you the true source of your feelings.
- If you can, plan a twenty-four-hour retreat somewhere so that you can enjoy an extended period of time alone with Jesus during your fast. These times of solitude with the Lord can be some of the most refreshing and liberating you will ever experience.
- Don't let failure to keep one fast become an excuse from trying again. If you find it difficult to keep a twenty-four-hour fast, try a twelve-hour one. If you find it difficult to keep a twelve-hour fast, try six hours. Any time dedicated to the Lord with an honest and humble heart will reap spiritual benefits.
- Give fasting the same regard in your life that you dedicate to prayer and giving. Remember that Jesus treated these three disciplines the same way.
- Incorporate a once-a-week fast into your life. Many people see God move in mighty ways in their lives once they begin a regular practice of this discipline.
- Most important, live in the joyous freedom purchased for you by Jesus Christ. Fasting is important, but living your life in sacrificial service to others is more important. Never let the fast keep you from living out the servant life modeled for you by your Lord.

APPENDIX B

RECOMMENDED READING

Bright, Bill. *The Coming Revival: America's Call to Fast, Pray, and "Seek God's Face."* Orlando: New Life Publications, 1995.

Christenson, Evelyn. *What Happens When Women Pray.* Colorado Springs, CO: Chariot/Victor, 1992.

Foster, Richard. *Celebration of Discipline: The Path to Spiritual Growth (25th Anniversary Edition).* New York: HarperCollins, 1998. (See especially the chapter on fasting.)

Murry, Andrew. *With Christ in the School of Prayer.* Springdale, PA: Whitaker, 1981.

Piper, John. *A Hunger for God: Desiring God Through Fasting and Prayer.* Wheaton, IL: Crossway, 1997.

Smith, Alice. *Beyond the Veil: Entering into Intimacy with God Through Prayer.* Ventura, CA: Gospel Light, 1997.

Towns, Elmer L. *Fasting for Spiritual Breakthrough: A Guide to Nine Spiritual Fasts.* Ventura, CA: Regal, 1996.

NOTES

1. Dr. Elisabeth Kübler-Ross's book *On Death and Dying* (New York: Simon & Schuster, 1969) describes stages that the terminally ill patient goes through as he or she progresses through illness toward death. Her book is considered a masterwork on the issue of healthy attitudes toward dying.

2. Foster, Richard. *Celebration of Discipline: The Path to Spiritual Growth (25th Anniversary Edition)* (New York: HarperCollins, 1998), 57.

3. Ignatius of Loyola encouraged believers to seek the nearness of God rather than practice harsh physical displays of penance. In a letter to Francisco de Borja, Duke of Gandia, dated September 20, 1548, Ignatius said that the gift of tears "could arise (1) because of our own sins or the sins of others; or (2) while contemplating the mysteries of the life of Christ, either here on earth or in heaven; or (3) from a loving consideration of the three Divine Persons." See "Selected Letters of St. Ignatius of Loyola," http://www.georgetown.edu/centers/woodstock/ignatius/letter11.htm.

4. See Dr. Don Colbert's excellent book *Fasting Made Easy* (Lake Mary, FL: Siloam Press, 2004) for a Christian perspective on the health benefits of fasting.

5. Michael Card, *Scribbling in the Sand: Christ and Creativity* (Downers Grove, IL: InterVarsity, 2002), 76.

6. John Rippon, "How Firm a Foundation" (1787), http://www.cyberhymnal.org/htm/h/f/hfirmafo.htm.

7. The few commands to fast given in the Bible are given by humans at times of national crisis. Esther requested that the Jewish people fast before she approached her husband, King Ahasuerus, to spare the lives of Jews threatened with annihilation (see Esther 4:16). The king of Nineveh made a similar plea when Jonah informed the city of the imminent judgment of God against the city because of its evil acts (see Jonah 3:5). These fasts were successful: In each case, God spared the people from harm.

ABOUT THE AUTHOR

CYNTHIA MOE lives in central Minnesota with her husband, Tim, and a menagerie of pets. She and Tim have raised three children and look forward to the eventual arrival of grandchildren.

Cynthia has worked as a freelance writer since 1993. *Hunger Pains* is her first book. She is currently at work on her second book, a novel titled *Fool's Lake*, which will be released in 2007. She is also a frequent public speaker and workshop leader on the topics of prayer and fasting.

LEARN TO BECOME THE WOMAN YOU WERE MEANT TO BE.